STAR WARS
EVEN MORE
CROCHET

LUCY COLLIN

An Hachette UK Company
www.hachette.co.uk

First published in Great Britain in 2017 by
ILEX, a division of Octopus Publishing Group Ltd
Octopus Publishing Group
Carmelite House
50 Victoria Embankment
London, EC4Y 0DZ
www.octopusbooks.co.uk

Disney | LUCASFILM © & TM 2017 Lucasfilm Ltd.
www.starwars.com

Produced by becker&mayer! LLC
Bellevue, Washington

www.beckermayer.com

Designer: Rosebud Eustace
Editor: Delia Greve
Photographer: Joseph Lambert
Production coordinator: Jennifer Marx
Product development: Peter Schumacher

All rights reserved. No part of this work may
be reproduced or utilised in any form or by
any means, electronic or mechanical, including
photocopying, recording or by any information
storage and retrieval system, without the prior
written permission of the publisher.

This book is part of the Star Wars Even More
Crochet kit and is not to be sold separately.

ISBN 978-1-78157-561-1

A CIP catalogue record for this book is
available from the British Library

Printed and bound in China

10 9 8 7 6 5 4 3 2 1

CONTENTS

Introduction 4
What's Included 4
Abbreviation Chart 5
Notes 6
Techniques and Terminology 7

PROJECT 1: JAWA 16

PROJECT 2: BB-8 20

PROJECT 3: REY 24

PROJECT 4: FINN 30

PROJECT 5: POE DAMERON 34

PROJECT 6: KYLO REN 40

PROJECT 7: OBI-WAN KENOBI 46

PROJECT 8: LANDO CALRISSIAN 52

PROJECT 9: ADMIRAL ACKBAR 56

PROJECT 10: NIEN NUNB 60

PROJECT 11: CANTINA BAND 64

PROJECT 12: GREEDO 70

About the Author 76
Acknowledgements 76

Introduction

It's been a great pleasure designing even more crochet patterns for this second *Star Wars* book. There are so many denizens of the *Star Wars* universe, it was hard to know which ones to transform into cute amigurumi figures. I wanted to do justice to major characters from the original trilogy who did not make it into the first kit, while also including some of the more popular minor characters. And like many fans, I fell instantly in love with *The Force Awakens* and all its wonderful new characters.

I hope you'll enjoy making these new crochet characters for all the *Star Wars* fans you know as much as I enjoyed creating them.

What's Included

This kit contains the materials you will need to make BB-8 and a Jawa. Included are the following: a size 3.5 mm crochet hook; a metal tapestry needle; yarn in black, dark brown, light brown, grey, white, and orange; two black and two amber plastic safety eyes; stuffing.

Abbreviation Chart

ch	chain
st	stitch or stitches
sl st	slip stitch
dc	double crochet
htr	half-treble
tr	treble
bob	bobble (see Special Stitch Instructions, page 14)
pop	popcorn stitch (see Special Stitch Instructions, page 14)
spike	spike stitch (see Special Stitch Instructions, page 14)
tog	together
dc2tog	decrease by working two dc together
BLO	back loop only
FLO	front loop only
FO	fasten off
YO	yarn over

Notes

ABOUT THIS KIT
All twelve featured figures are made in rounds from the top of the head down, with parts such as arms and ears made separately. Do not join rounds. Work through both loops of stitches unless otherwise indicated.

All the figures that have visible legs are crocheted with a solid bottom half. This is then divided to make legs by threading a length of yarn back and forth through the middle. Full details of how to do this are included in each relevant pattern.

YARN
These figures have been made using double knitting weight yarn, but you can also use aran weight yarn. It is best to use the same weight of yarn throughout a project and to stick to the same brand of yarn if possible. The amounts given in each pattern are approximate and may vary depending on the type of yarn used, so make sure you get enough yarn to complete each project. The patterns work best if you use acrylic yarn or acrylic with some wool content.

STITCH MARKERS
Using a stitch marker to indicate the start of a round can be helpful. You can buy plastic ones or use paper clips or safety pins; you can also use a small piece of contrasting yarn. You will also need a clip-type stitch marker to secure the working loop when you set a project aside. It is best to place the marker under the stitch at the start of the round.

SMALL PLIERS
A pair of small, flat-nosed pliers that are used in crafts such as jewellery-making are useful when you're sewing parts together. Pliers can be used to grasp the needle and pull it through if necessary.

PINS
Long, round-headed pins are helpful to secure parts when you're sewing them together.

Techniques and Terminology

If you are new to crochet, here are the basics you'll need to know for this book. Making amigurumi (toys worked in the round) is a bit different from making other items using crochet, so if you've never made them before, be sure to read all the instructions so you understand the techniques.

SLIPKNOT
Most crochet starts with a slipknot. Make a circle of yarn a short distance from the end of the piece of yarn and loop over your hook, then tighten into a knot so that the loop moves freely on your hook. (Figs. A & B)

YARN OVER (YO)
To make every stitch, you need to pass the yarn over the hook. Hold the hook in your right hand (if you are right-handed) between your thumb and index finger and lightly clasp the short end of yarn in the rest of your fingers. Hold the rest of the yarn in your left hand, catching it around the back of your index finger, and pass it around the back of the hook and over the front so it gets caught in the hook at the end.

CHAIN STITCH (CH)
YO, catch hold of the short end of yarn with your left thumb and middle finger, and pull the yarn through the loop on the hook. This makes one chain stitch – it's a good idea to practise this a lot to get used to holding the hook and yarn. (Fig. C–page 8)

WORKING INTO THE CHAIN
To work into the chain, turn the chain and start working into it from the end nearest the hook. If you look at the chain, you will see that each

Fig. A

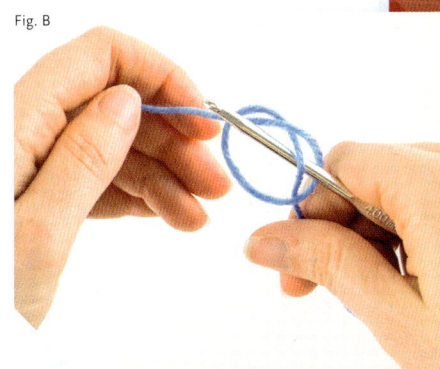

Fig. B

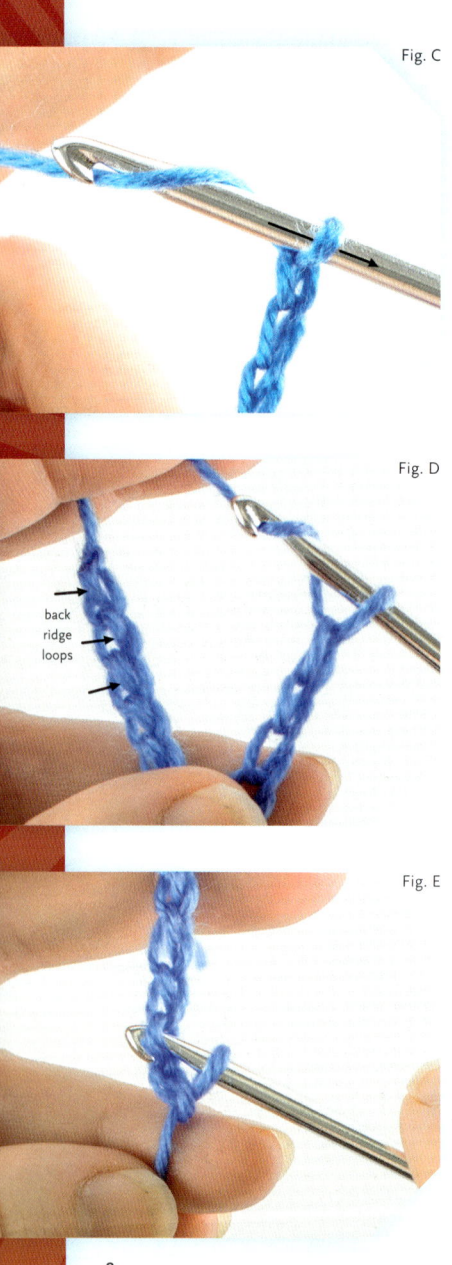

Fig. C

Fig. D

back ridge loops

Fig. E

chain stitch consists of two lines making a sideways "v" shape, with another line behind them (the back ridge loops – Fig. D). You usually skip the chain nearest the hook (this is always stated in the patterns) and then push the hook between the "v" and below the back ridge loops. (Fig. E)

When making amigurumi, you do not need to work into the chain very often, but you should learn how as you will need to do it when you make Obi-Wan's robe, Finn's jacket, and other parts that are worked in rows rather than rounds.

WORKING INTO A STITCH

All stitches are the same at the top; they have two lines that make a sideways "v" shape. Each of these lines is called a loop. To work into a stitch, insert your hook under both loops from the front to the back.

BACK LOOP ONLY (BLO)

Insert your hook under the back loop of the two loops (the one farthest away from you as you are facing your work) that make the stitch you are working into. Continue with the stitch as normal. (Fig. F)

FRONT LOOP ONLY (FLO)

Insert your hook under the front loop of the two loops (the closest one to you as you are facing your work), that make the top of the stitch you are working into. Continue with the stitch as normal.

SLIP STITCH (SL ST)

This is a very flat stitch that is not used often, but is sometimes necessary to tidy up your work. Push the hook into the ch or st, YO (Fig. G), pull through ch or st and loop on hook.

DOUBLE CROCHET (DC)

This is the stitch you will use most of the time when making amigurumi. Push the hook into the ch or st, YO, pull through ch or st, YO (Fig. H), pull through both loops on hook.

HALF-TREBLE (HTR)

This is a slightly taller stitch than a sc. YO, push hook into ch or st, YO (Fig. I–page 10), pull through ch or st, YO, pull through three loops on hook.

TREBLE (TR)

This stitch is about twice as tall as a sc. YO, push hook into ch or st, YO, pull through ch or st (Fig. J–page 10), YO, pull through two loops on hook, YO, pull through remaining two loops on hook.

INCREASING AND DECREASING

To make what you're crocheting larger or smaller, you increase or decrease. To increase, work two stitches (in these patterns that will always be dc) into the same stitch or chain. (Fig. K–page 10) To decrease,

Fig. F

Fig. G

Fig. H

Fig. I

Fig. J

Fig. K

work into two stitches at once and end up with only one stitch, as described next with a dc2tog.

DOUBLE CROCHET TWO TOGETHER (DC2TOG)

Push hook into st, YO and pull through st, push hook into next st, YO and pull through st, YO and pull through three loops on hook. (Fig. L)

INVISIBLE DECREASE

This gives a neater look when you decrease, so it is especially good to use on faces. Push hook through the front loop of st, push hook through the front loop of next st, YO and pull through two loops on hook, YO and pull through two remaining loops on hook.

FASTEN OFF (FO)

When you finish a piece of crochet, cut the yarn, leaving a length of about 30cm (or however much the pattern calls for) and pull this yarn through the stitch. This yarn will then be used to sew pieces together, or it will be sewn through the fabric to secure the yarn (see Weave In Ends, page 14).

ROWS

To make a flat piece of crocheted fabric, make a chain of a certain length then work into that chain. Turn your work at the end of the row and continue with the next row in the opposite direction. Continue working rows backward and forward as necessary for the pattern. (Fig. M)

ROUNDS (RND)

To make a three-dimensional piece of crochet, such as the figures in this book, work a number of stitches into one stitch (see also Adjustable Ring, below), making a small circle. Continue with the next round by working the next stitch into the first stitch of the first round and so on around the circle (with increases if necessary). (Fig. N) These rounds are continuous, so you will not be able to see the start of each round unless you mark it. Use a stitch marker or a small piece of contrasting yarn.

STARTING THE FIRST ROUND

Ch 2, then work the number of dc in the first round (generally six) into the first ch. Work the dc over the tail of yarn as well and use that to pull the hole tight.

ADJUSTABLE RING

This is an alternative way to start the first round. Make a loop around the first and second fingers of your right hand. Remove it from your fingers and put the hook through the loop. (Fig. O–page 12) YO and pull through. YO and pull through loop on hook, pulling tight. Then work the number of dc in the first round around the loop of yarn. (Fig. P–page 12) At the end of the first round, pull the end of the yarn tight to make a neat circle with no hole in the middle.

Fig. L

Fig. M

Fig. N

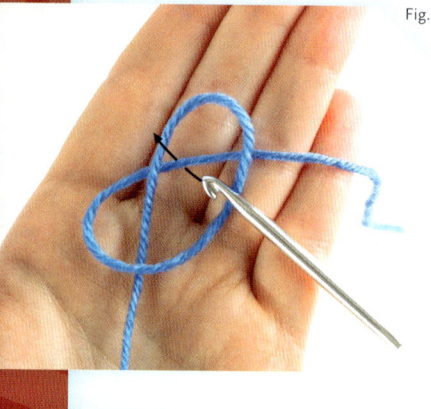

Fig. O

Fig. P

RIGHT SIDE AND WRONG SIDE

When working in rows, there isn't always a clear right or wrong side to the fabric. When working in rounds, however, there is an obvious inside and outside. As you start to crochet a rounded shape, the side that is facing you as you work is the right side. As the fabric becomes bowl-shaped, it should be on the other side of your hook as you are crocheting. If you are working inside-out, your work will be between you and your hook. You can see the difference between the two sides – the right side (outside) is smoother and has distinct lines between the rounds that you can easily count. The wrong side (inside) has a rougher texture and less distinct lines. (Fig. Q)

When you are working on a small part, like an arm, it is easy to end up working inside out. After a few rounds use the blunt end of your

RIGHT SIDE   WRONG SIDE

Fig. Q

crochet hook to push the part the right way around. While there's nothing bad in general about crocheting wrong-side out, some elements of the pattern may not work or may look strange.

TENSION

When crocheting in the round to make amigurumi, you need to crochet each stitch quite tightly so that the fabric won't stretch to let the stuffing show through – but not so tightly that you can't work into the stitches on the next round. When you make pieces in rows, such as the Jawa's hood, you can work a bit more loosely.

CHANGING YARN COLOURS

When changing from one colour of yarn to another, work up to the change until there are two loops left on the hook. Then use the new colour for the final YO and pull through. Work a few dc over the tails of the end of the old yarn and the start of the new yarn to secure them. For places where there is a change to a new colour and then back to the original one in the same row, carry the colour you are not using behind your work by working over it every three stitches so that the colour does not show through – but be careful not to pull the carried yarn too tight or it will affect the shape of the figure. (Fig. R)

Fig. R

Fig. S

Fig. T

Fig. U

Fig. V

Fig. W

CONSTRUCTION
Use yarn tails from the completed pieces to sew on parts such as arms. Pin the smaller piece to the larger piece and sew through the top of each stitch on the smaller piece into the larger piece.

WEAVE IN ENDS
When you work in rounds, most of the ends of yarn get left on the inside of the figure, so you don't need to worry about them. On flat pieces, you need to tidy up any loose ends by sewing through a few stitches and back again to keep the ends from unraveling.

JOINING IN YARN
To join new yarn to your work, put your hook through the stitch as indicated in the instructions and pull a loop of new yarn through. YO and pull through loop on hook. Tighten. When you continue with the instructions, start in the same stitch.

SPECIAL STITCH INSTRUCTIONS
BOBBLE STITCH, 2TR (2TR BOB): YO, insert hook into next stitch, YO and pull through loop (Fig. S–page 13), YO, pull through two loops, YO, insert hook into same stitch, YO and pull through loop, YO, pull through two loops, YO, pull through all three loops on hook. (Fig. T–page 13)

BOBBLE STITCH, 3TR (3TR BOB): YO, insert hook into next stitch, YO and pull through loop (Fig. U), YO, pull through two loops, *YO, insert hook into same stitch, YO and pull through loop, YO, pull through two loops, repeat once from *, YO, pull through all four loops on hook. (Fig. V)

POPCORN STITCH, 3TR (3TR POP): Work 3tr into one st, remove hook from working loop, push through both loops of first tr and pull working loop through. (Fig. W)

SPIKE STITCH, DC (SPIKE DC) Insert hook into space between stitches one row/round below working stitches, YO, pull through space between stitches, YO, pull through both loops on hook. (Fig. X)

Fig. X

PROJECT 1

JAWA

FINISHED SIZE: approximately 9 cm tall

These little scavengers live on the desert planet of Tatooine. Travelling around in gigantic sandcrawlers, they are constantly on the lookout for junk, scrap metal from crashed starships or lost droids, which they repair and sell to local townsfolk and farmers.

MATERIALS
See note on yarn, p. 6

- Black yarn (approx. 10 g)
- Dark brown yarn (approx. 15 g)
- Small amount of slightly lighter brown yarn for feet and shoulder strap
- 3.5 mm hook
- Tapestry needle
- Pair of amber, yellow, or orange plastic safety eyes (9 mm)
- Stuffing
- Stitch marker

HEAD AND BODY: Start with black yarn.

Rnd 1: ch 2, work 6 dc into first ch – 6 st.

Rnd 2: 2 dc in each st around – 12 st.

Rnd 3: [2 dc in next st, dc in next st] 6 times – 18 st.

Rnd 4: [2 dc in next st, dc in next 2 st] 6 times – 24 st.

Rnds 5–9: (5 rounds) dc in each st around—24 st.

Rnd 10: [sc2tog, sc in next 2 st] 6 times – 18 st.

• Fit eyes between rounds 7 and 8, five stitches apart, with the start of the rounds placed at the back of the Jawa.

Rnd 11: [dc2tog, dc in next st] 6 times – 12 st.

• Change to brown yarn.

Rnd 12: [2 dc in next st, dc in next 3 st] 3 times – 15 st.

Rnd 13: [2 dc in next st, dc in next 4 st] 3 times – 18 st.

Rnds 14–16: (3 rounds) dc in each st around – 18 st.

Rnd 17: [2 dc in next st, dc in next 5 st] 3 times – 21 st.

Rnd 18: dc in each st around – 21 st.

Rnd 19: [2 dc in next st, dc in next 6 st] 3 times – 24 st.

Rnd 20: dc in each st around – 24 st.

Rnd 21: [2 dc in next st, dc in next 7 st] 3 times – 27 st.

Rnd 22: dc in each st around – 27 st.

• Stuff head firmly.

• Change to lighter brown yarn.

To mark the feet: Find the stitch in round 22 that is in the front middle of the body. Then count back six stitches before that (not including the middle stitch) and mark this stitch.

Rnd 23: in BLO for the whole round, dc in each st around until you get to the marked stitch.

To make feet: Work a 3tr bob in each of next 4 st, dc in next 5 st, work a 3tr bob in each of next 4 st. Dc in each st around to the end of the round – 27 st.

Fig. A

Fig. B

Fig. C

Fig. D

- Make sure the bobbles that make up the feet are pushed outward.
- Stuff body.

Rnd 24: [dc2tog, dc in next st] 9 times – 18 st.

Rnd 25: [dc2tog, dc in next st] 6 times – 12 st.

Rnd 26: [dc2tog] 6 times – 6 st. FO, leaving a length of yarn.

- Finish stuffing firmly, then sew the hole at the base up neatly and pull the yarn up tightly through the body to make sure the base lies flat. Take the yarn through the body again (not tightly) and then cut it.

HOOD: Brown yarn.

- Ch 24.

Row 1: dc in second ch from hook, dc in next 22 ch, ch 1, turn – 23 st.

Rows 2–9: (8 rows) dc in next 23 st, ch 1, turn – 23 st.

Row 10: dc2tog, dc in next 19 st, dc2tog, ch 1, turn – 21 st.

Row 11: dc2tog, dc in next 17 st, dc2tog – 19 st.

- FO, leaving length of yarn.
- Fold in half and, using the length of yarn, sew up the back of the hood along the sides of rows 10 and 11 and then along the top of row 11.
- Weave the yarn back through the hood until it comes out at the start of the sewn-up back, then turn the hood inside out (Fig. A–page 17). Pin to the neck, with this point at the back, and rows 1 and 2 sticking out (Fig. B–page 17). Sew to the neck, and sew the edges of rounds 1 and 2 so the hood is a tube shape at the front. (Fig. C) Weave in any loose ends.

ARMS (make 2): Start with black yarn.

Rnd 1: ch 2, work 6 dc into first ch – 6 st.

Rnd 2: dc in each st around – 6 st.

- Change to brown yarn.

Rnd 3: [2 dc in next st, dc in next st] 3 times – 9 st.

Rnds 4–5: (2 rounds) dc in each st around – 9 st.

Rnd 6: dc2tog, dc in next 7 st – 8 st.

Rnd 7: dc in each st around – 8 st.

Rnd 8: [dc2tog, dc in next 2 st] 2 times – 6 st. Sl st in next st, then FO, leaving a length of yarn.

• Sew the arms to the body.

SHOULDER STRAP: Lighter brown yarn.

• Ch 22.

• Dc in second ch from hook, dc in next 13 ch, [2tr bob in next ch, dc in next ch] 3 times, dc in next ch – 21 st.

• FO, leaving a length of yarn. Place across body with the three bobble stitches (pouches) at the front, sew ends together, and secure to body in two or three places. Secure any loose ends. (Fig. D)

PROJECT 2

BB-8

FINISHED SIZE: approximately 7 cm tall

This little astromech droid co-pilots for Poe Dameron's starfighter for the Resistance. After being left on Jakku, BB-8 is found by Rey and becomes an essential part of her adventure with Finn.

MATERIALS
See note on yarn, p. 6

- White yarn (approx. 15 g)
- Light grey yarn (approx. 5 g)
- Orange yarn (approx. 5 g)
- 3.5 mm hook
- Tapestry needle
- 9 mm black plastic safety eye
- 6 mm black plastic safety eye
- Stuffing
- Stitch marker

BODY: Start with light grey yarn.

Rnd 1: ch 2, work 6 dc into first ch—6 st.

• Change to white yarn.

Rnd 2: 2 dc in each st around – 12 st.

• Change to orange yarn.

Rnd 3: [dc in next st, dc and spike st in next st, dc in next st] 4 times – 16 st.

• Change to white yarn.

Rnd 4: [2 dc in next st, dc in next st] 8 times – 24 st.

Rnd 5: [2 dc in next st, dc in next 3 st] 6 times – 30 st.

Rnds 6–13: (8 rounds) dc in each st around – 30 st.

Rnd 14: [dc2tog, dc in next 3 st] 6 times – 24 st.

• Change to orange yarn.

Rnd 15: [dc2tog, dc in next st] 8 times – 16 st.

• Start to stuff body.

• Change to white yarn.

Rnd 16: [dc2tog, dc in next 2 st] 4 times – 12 st.

• Change to light grey yarn.

Rnd 17: [dc2tog] 6 times – 6 st. FO, leaving a length of yarn.

• Finish stuffing firmly, then neatly sew up the hole at the base. (Completed body, top: Fig. A, bottom: Fig. B)

CIRCULAR PANELS (make 4): Start with light grey yarn.

Rnd 1: ch 2, work 6 dc into first ch – 6 st.

• Change to white yarn.

Rnd 2: 2 dc in each st around – 12 st.

• Change to orange yarn.

Fig. A

Fig. B

Fig. C

Fig. D

Fig. E

Rnd 3: [dc in next st, dc and spike st in next st, dc in next st] 4 times – 16 st.

- Change to white yarn.

Rnd 4: [2 dc in next st, dc in next st] 8 times – 24 st. Sl st in next st. FO, leaving a length of yarn.

- Secure and trim all the ends.

- Pin each panel in place on the white part of the body so that they are equally spaced. Sew neatly around the edges, making sure that they are as flat as possible. (Fig. C– page 21)

HEAD: Start with white yarn.

Rnd 1: ch 2, work 6 dc into first ch – 6 st.

- Change to light grey yarn.

Rnd 2: 2 dc in each st around – 12 st.

- Change to white yarn.

Rnd 3: [2 dc in next st, dc in next st] 6 times – 18 st.

Rnd 4: [2 dc in next st, dc in next 5 st] 3 times – 21 st.

Rnds 5–6: (2 rounds) dc in each st around – 21 st.

Fig. F

- Change to light grey yarn.

Rnd 7: dc in each st around – 21 st.

- Change to white yarn.

Rnd 8: in BLO, [dc2tog, dc in next 5 st] 3 times – 18 st.

- Secure your current loop with a stitch marker so your work doesn't come undone.

- With the start of the round at the back, insert the 9 mm eye at the front, between rounds 4 and 5. Insert the 6 mm eye between rounds 5 and 6, three stitches to the right as you are facing it. (Fig. D) Do not secure the eyes with the washers on the back yet.

• To make the orange lines on the head, you will work slip stitches along the surface into the holes between stitches.

• Insert your hook between rounds 3 and 4, two stitches to the right of the larger eye as you are facing it. Pull a loop of orange yarn from underneath and through the hole, then work 14 sl st around in a circle, pulling the yarn from underneath for each stitch. Finish one stitch away from the larger eye on the other side. FO and weave in the ends on the inside.

• Insert your hook between rounds 6 and 7, one stitch to the right of the smaller eye as you are facing it. Pull a loop of orange yarn from underneath and through the hole, then work 16 sl st around in a circle, pulling the yarn from underneath for each stitch. (Fig. E) Finish one stitch away from the larger eye on the other side. FO and weave in the ends on the inside.

• Fix the washers on the backs of the safety eyes. (Fig. F)

• Stuff head.

Rnd 9: [dc2tog, dc in next st] 6 times – 12 st.

Rnd 10: [dc2tog] 6 times – 6 st. FO, leaving a length of yarn.

• Finish stuffing, then sew the hole up neatly. Sew head onto body so that the edge of the head is touching the middle of round 1. Do not sew into the grey part of the head; sew into round 8 of the head.

PROJECT
3

REY

FINISHED SIZE: approximately 9.5 cm tall

Left on the desert planet of Jakku, Rey becomes skilled in survival, combat and working with machinery. Her piloting skills allow her to help Finn escape the First Order and provide the Resistance with information on the location of Luke Skywalker. Tapping into an unknown affinity with the Force, Rey defends herself from Kylo Ren and goes in search of Luke Skywalker.

MATERIALS
See note on yarn, p. 6

- Brown yarn (approx. 10 g)
- Pale peach yarn (approx. 10 g)
- Light beige yarn (approx. 15 g)
- Dark beige yarn (approx. 5 g)
- Small amount of slightly lighter brown yarn (for belt)
- Small amount of bright blue and light grey yarn (for lightsaber)
- Small amount of black embroidery thread (for mouth)
- 3.5 mm hook
- 4.0 mm hook
- Tapestry needle
- Pair of black plastic safety eyes (7.5 mm)
- Stuffing
- Drinking straw
- Stitch marker

HEAD AND BODY: Start with brown yarn.

Rnd 1: ch 2, work 6 dc into first ch – 6 st.

Rnd 2: 2 dc in each st around – 12 st.

Rnd 3: [2 dc in next st, dc in next st] 6 times – 18 st.

Rnd 4: [2 dc in next st, dc in next 2 st] 6 times – 24 st.

Rnd 5: dc in next 16 st, (sl st in next st, ch 6, dc in second ch from hook, dc in next 4 ch, sl st back into same st on round), dc in next 7 st – 24 st.

• For rounds following ones with the sticking-out piece of hair, work into the first sl st, take the yarn under the hair, skip the second sl st and then work into the next st on the round.

Rnd 6: dc in each st around – 24 st.

Rnd 7: *change to pale peach yarn*, dc in next 10 st, *change to brown yarn*, dc in next 14 st – 24 st.

Rnd 8: *change to pale peach yarn*, dc in next 11 st, *change to brown yarn*, dc in next 5 st, (sl st in next st, ch 6, dc in second ch from hook, sc in next 4 ch, sl st back into same st on round), dc in next 6 st, *change to pale peach yarn*, dc in next st – 24 st.

Rnd 9: dc in next 12 st, *change to brown yarn*, dc in next 11 st, *change to pale peach yarn*, dc in next st – 24 st.

Rnd 10: dc in next 12 st, *change to brown yarn*, dc in next 10 st, *change to pale peach yarn*, dc in next 2 st – 24 st.

Rnd 11: dc in next 13 st, *change to brown yarn*, dc in next 4 st, (sl st in next st, ch 8, dc in second ch from hook, dc in next 6 ch, sl st back into same st on round), dc in next 4 st,

Fig. A

Fig. B

Fig. C

Fig. D

Fig. E

Fig. F

change to pale peach yarn, dc in next 2 st – 24 st. (Leave a length of brown yarn when you cut it.)

Rnd 12: [dc2tog, dc in next 2 st] 6 times – 18 st.

- Fit eyes between rounds 9 and 10, six stitches apart.

Rnd 13: [dc2tog, dc in next st] 6 times – 12 st.

- Change to light beige yarn.

Rnd 14: dc in each st around – 12 st.

Rnd 15: [2 dc in next st, dc in next 3 st] 3 times – 15 st.

Rnds 16–17: (2 rounds) dc in each st around – 15 st.

Rnd 18: [2 dc in next st, dc in next 4 st] 3 times – 18 st.

- Stuff head, and sew a mouth with black thread.

- Using length of brown yarn, sew the ends of each sticking-out piece of hair into the top of each piece and into the head to make a loop. (Fig. A–page 25)

- Change to lighter brown yarn.

Rnd 19: dc in each st around – 18 st.

- Change to dark beige yarn.

Rnd 20: in BLO, dc in each st around – 18 st.

Rnd 21: [2 dc in next st, dc in next 5 st] 3 times – 21 st.

Rnd 22: dc in each st around – 21 st.

Rnd 23: [2 dc in next st, dc in next 6 st] 3 times – 24 st.

- Change to pale peach yarn, leaving a piece of dark beige yarn about 40 cm long when you cut it.

Rnd 24: dc in each st around – 24 st.

Rnd 25: [2 dc in next st, dc in next 7 st] 3 times – 27 st.

- Change to brown yarn.

Rnds 26–27: (2 rounds) dc in each st around – 27 st.

To mark the feet: Find the stitch in round 27 that is in the front middle of the body. Then count back six stitches before that (not including the middle stitch) and mark this stitch.

Rnd 28: dc in each st around until you get to the marked stitch.

To make feet: Work a 3tr bob in each of next 4 st, dc in next 5 st, work a 3tr bob in each of next 4 st. Dc in each st around to the end of the round – 27 st.

- Make sure the bobbles that make up the feet are pushed outward.
- Stuff top half of body firmly.

Rnd 29: [dc2tog, dc in next st] 9 times – 18 st.

Rnd 30: [dc2tog, dc in next st] 6 times – 12 st.

Rnd 31: [dc2tog] 6 times – 6 st. FO, leaving a length of yarn.

- Thread the length of dark beige yarn out at the middle front of Rey at the top of round 22.
- Finish stuffing; stuff slightly less firmly below the waist.
- Neatly sew up the hole at the base with the length of brown yarn and pull the yarn up through the body tightly to make sure the base lies flat before cutting the brown yarn.
- To define the legs, take the dark beige yarn sticking out at the front middle, sew through the body from the top of round 23 to the top of round 22 at the middle back, and pull tightly. Go down one round, then sew the yarn back through to the front and again pull tightly. Continue to do this, working down the legs round by round, until you reach the base of the figure. Take the yarn through the base (not tightly) a couple of times to secure and then cut it.

FABRIC PANELS BELOW BELT (make 4): Light beige yarn.

- Ch 6.

Row 1: dc in second ch from hook, dc in next 4 ch, ch 1, turn – 5 st.

Row 2: dc in next 5 st, ch 1, turn – 5 st.

Row 3: dc in next 5 st – 5 st. FO, leaving length of yarn.

- Sew in place under the belt, two at the front and two at the back. (Figs. B & C–page 25)

Fig. G

Fig. H

ARMS (make 2): Start with pale peach yarn.

Rnd 1: ch 2, work 6 dc into first ch – 6 st.

Rnd 2: dc in each st around – 6 st.

• Change to lighter brown yarn for left arm, light beige yarn for right arm.

Rnd 3: [2dc in next st, dc in next 2 st] 2 times – 8 st.

• Change to (or continue with) light beige yarn.

• Work in BLO for right arm only on next round.

Rnd 4: dc in each st around – 8 st.

Rnds 5–7: (3 rounds) in BLO, dc in each st around – 8 st.

• Change to pale peach yarn.

Rnd 8: [dc2tog, dc in next 2 st] 2 times – 6 st.

Rnd 9: dc in each st around – 6 st. Sl st in next st, then FO, leaving a length of yarn.

• Stuff the ends of the arms slightly, then sew the arms to the body.

HEADGEAR: Light beige yarn.

Use 4.0 mm hook or work more loosely.

Rnd 1: ch 2, work 6 dc into first ch – 6 st.

Rnd 2: 2 dc in each st around – 12 st.

Rnd 3: [2 dc in next st, dc in next st] 6 times – 18 st.

Rnd 4: [2 dc in next st, dc in next 2 st] 6 times – 24 st.

Rnds 5–7: (3 rounds) dc in each st around – 24 st.

Rnd 8: 2tr bob in each st around – 24 st.

Rnd 9: dc in next 12 st, sl st in next 12 st – 24 st.

Row 10: dc in next 12 st, ch 1, turn.

Row 11: dc in next 12 st, ch 5, turn.

Row 12: dc in next 12 st, ch 35, turn.

Row 13: htr in third ch from hook, htr in next 32 st, sl st into side of previous row. FO and weave in end.

GOGGLES: Light beige yarn.

Use 4.0 mm hook or work more loosely.

- Ch 6, sl st to join to first ch to form loop, ch 8, sl st into sixth ch from hook to form second loop.

- Dc in next 2 ch, 10 dc around first loop, dc in back of 2 ch, 10 dc around second loop.

- Sl st all around the outside of the goggles (24 st). FO, leaving length of yarn. Sew each end to the headgear over round 8. (Fig. D – page 26)

- To fasten the headgear around Rey's head, pass the long strand through the loop (Fig. E – page 26) and wrap all the way around the neck. Tuck the loose end under the strand at the back. (Fig. F – page 26)

LIGHTSABER: Start with bright blue yarn.

Rnd 1: ch 2, work 6 dc into first ch – 6 st.

Rnds 2–10: (9 rounds) dc in each st around – 6 st.

- Change to light grey yarn.

Rnds 11–14: (4 rounds) dc in each st around – 6 st. FO, leaving a length of yarn.

- Cut a length of drinking straw to fit inside the lightsaber (if the straw is too wide, cut along it lengthways and roll it so it is thinner), and insert it. (Fig. G)

- Sew up the end neatly and sew to Rey's hand if you wish. (Fig. H)

PROJECT 4

Finn

FINISHED SIZE: approximately 9.5cm tall

Despite having trained his whole life to be a stormtrooper, Finn is horrified by the brutality he witnesses on Jakku, and he helps Poe escape the First Order. After meeting Rey and Han Solo, he soon finds himself caught up with the Resistance.

MATERIALS
See note on yarn, p. 6

- Black yarn (approx. 15 g)
- Light brown yarn (approx. 5 g)
- Dark grey yarn (approx. 5 g)
- Honey-brown yarn (approx. 10 g)
- Small amount of russet yarn
- Small amount of black embroidery thread (for mouth)
- 3.5 mm hook
- Tapestry needle
- Pair of black plastic safety eyes (7.5 mm)
- Stuffing
- Stitch marker

HEAD AND BODY: Start with black yarn.

Rnd 1: ch 2, work 6 dc into first ch – 6 st.

Rnd 2: 2 dc in each st around – 12 st.

Rnd 3: [2 dc in next st, dc in next st] 6 times – 18 st.

Rnd 4: [2 dc in next st, dc in next 2 st] 6 times – 24 st.

Rnds 5–6: (2 rounds) dc in each st around – 24 st.

Rnd 7: *change to light brown yarn*, dc in next 9 st, *change to black yarn*, dc in next 15 st – 24 st.

Rnd 8: *change to light brown yarn*, dc in next 9 st, *change to black yarn*, dc in next 15 st – 24 st.

Rnd 9: *change to light brown yarn*, dc in next 10 st, *change to black yarn*, dc in next 14 st – 24 st.

Rnd 10: *change to light brown yarn*, dc in next 11 st, *change to black yarn*, dc in next 12 st, *change to light brown yarn*, dc in next st – 24 st.

Rnd 11: dc in next 11 st, *change to black yarn*, dc in next 12 st, *change to light brown yarn*, dc in next st – 24 st.

Rnd 12: [dc2tog, dc in next 2 st] 6 times – 18 st.

• Fit eyes between rounds 9 and 10, six stitches apart.

Rnd 13: [dc2tog, dc in next st] 6 times – 12 st.

• Change to black yarn.

Rnd 14: [2 dc in next st, dc in next st] 6 times – 18 st.

Rnds 15–20: (6 rounds) dc in each st around – 18 st.

• Stuff head and sew a mouth with black thread.

Fig. A

Fig. B

Fig. C

Fig. D

Rnd 21: in BLO, [2 dc in next st, dc in next 5 st] 3 times – 21 st.

Rnd 22: dc in each st around – 21 st.

Rnd 23: [2 dc in next st, dc in next 6 st] 3 times – 24 st.

Rnd 24: dc in each st around – 24 st.

Rnd 25: [2 dc in next st, dc in next 7 st] 3 times – 27 st.

Rnd 26: dc in each st around – 27 st.

Fig. E

• Change to dark grey yarn, leaving a piece of black yarn about 40 cm long when you cut it.

Rnd 27: dc in each st around – 27 st.

To mark the feet: Find the stitch in round 27 that is in the front middle of the body. Then count back six stitches before that (not including the middle stitch) and mark this stitch.

Fig. F

Rnd 28: dc in each st around until you get to the marked stitch.

To make feet: Work a 3tr bob in each of next 4 st, dc in next 5 st, work a 3tr bob in each of next 4 st. Dc in each st around to the end of the round – 27 st.

• Make sure the bobbles that make up the feet are pushed outward.

• Stuff top half of body firmly.

Rnd 29: [dc2tog, dc in next st] 9 times – 18 st.

Fig. G

Rnd 30: [dc2tog, dc in next st] 6 times – 12 st.

Rnd 31: [dc2tog] 6 times – 6 st. FO, leaving a length of yarn.

• Thread the length of black yarn out at the middle front of Finn at the top of round 23.

• Finish stuffing; stuff slightly less firmly below the waist.

- Neatly sew up the hole at the base with the length of dark grey yarn and pull the yarn up through the body tightly to make sure the base lies flat before cutting the dark grey yarn.

- To define the legs, take the black yarn sticking out at the front middle, sew through the body from the top of round 24 to the top of round 23 at the middle back, and pull tightly. Go down one round, then sew the yarn back through to the front and again pull tightly. Continue to do this, working down the legs round by round, until you reach the base of the figure. Take the yarn through the base (not tightly) a couple of times to secure and then cut it. (Fig. A–page 31)

ARMS (make 2): Start with light brown yarn.

Rnd 1: ch 2, work 6 dc into first ch – 6 st.

Rnd 2: dc in each st around – 6 st.

- Change to black yarn.

Rnd 3: [2 dc in next st, dc in next 2 st] 2 times – 8 st.

Rnds 4–9: (6 rounds) dc in each st around – 8 st.

Rnd 10: [dc2tog, dc in next 2 st] 2 times – 6 st. Sl st in next st, then FO, leaving a length of yarn.

- Stuff the ends of the arms slightly, then sew the arms to the body.

JACKET: Start with honey-brown yarn.

- Ch 17.

Row 1: 2 dc in second ch from hook, dc in next 14 ch, *change to russet yarn, carrying honey-brown yarn underneath,* 2 dc in next ch, ch 1, turn – 18 st.

Row 2: dc in next 2 st, *change to honey-brown yarn,* ch 5, skip next 4 st, dc in next 6 st, ch 5, skip next 4 st, dc in next 2 st, ch 1, turn – 18 st.

Row 3: dc in next 2 st, work 5 dc around ch 5, dc in next 6 st, work 5 dc around ch 5, dc in next 2 st, ch 1, turn – 20 st. (Fig. B–page 31)

Rows 4–6: dc in next 20 st, ch 1, turn – 20 st.

Row 7: dc in next 20 st. FO.

- Weave in any loose ends.

SLEEVES (make 2):
Honey-brown yarn.

Holding jacket upside down with the outside facing you (russet patch at bottom left), join in yarn to first of skipped 4 st in armhole, leaving a length of yarn at start.

- Dc in each of 4 skipped st, ch 7. (Figs. C–page 31 & D)

Rnd 1: dc into first dc worked above to make a ring, dc in next 3 dc, work 8 dc around ch 7 – 12 st. (Fig. E)

Rnds 2–9: (8 rounds) dc in each st around – 12 st. (Fig. F)

- Dc in next st, FO.

- Use yarn from start to sew up the gap under each sleeve. Weave in any loose ends.

- Using the russet yarn, sew a double line on the front left of the jacket, opposite the russet patch. (Fig. G)

- Weave in any loose ends.

Poe Dameron

FINISHED SIZE: approximately 9.5 cm tall

An outstanding pilot and determined fighter who joined the Resistance to counter the threat of the First Order, Poe is captured and tortured by Kylo Ren. Rescued by Finn, Poe and his skills in an X-wing are essential in the Battle at Starkiller Base.

MATERIALS
See note on yarn, p. 6

- Dark brown yarn (approx. 5 g)
- Light beige yarn (approx. 5 g)
- Orange yarn (approx. 10 g)
- White yarn (approx. 5 g)
- Dark grey yarn (approx. 5 g)
- Black yarn (approx. 10 g)
- Red yarn (approx. 5 g)
- Small amount of light grey yarn (for uniform details)
- Small amount of black embroidery thread (for mouth)
- 3.5 mm hook
- Tapestry needle
- Pair of black plastic safety eyes (7.5 mm)
- Stuffing
- Stitch marker

HEAD AND BODY: Start with dark brown yarn.

Rnd 1: ch 2, work 6 dc into first ch – 6 st.

Rnd 2: 2 dc in each st around – 12 st.

Rnd 3: [2 dc in next st, dc in next st] 6 times – 18 st.

Rnd 4: [2 dc in next st, dc in next 2 st] 6 times – 24 st.

Rnds 5–6: (2 rounds) dc in each st around – 24 st.

Rnd 7: *change to light beige yarn*, dc in next 9 st, *change to dark brown yarn*, dc in next 15 st – 24 st.

Rnd 8: *change to light beige yarn*, dc in next 9 st, *change to dark brown yarn*, dc in next 15 st – 24 st.

Rnd 9: *change to light beige yarn*, dc in next 10 st, *change to dark brown yarn*, dc in next 14 st – 24 st.

Rnd 10: *change to light beige yarn*, dc in next 11 st, *change to dark brown yarn*, dc in next 12 st, *change to light beige yarn*, dc in next st – 24 st.

Rnd 11: dc in next 11 st, *change to dark brown yarn*, dc in next 12 st, *change to light beige yarn*, dc in next st – 24 st.

Rnd 12: [dc2tog, dc in next 2 st] 6 times – 18 st.

• Fit eyes between rounds 9 and 10, six stitches apart.

Rnd 13: [dc2tog, dc in next st] 6 times – 12 st.

• Change to white yarn.

Rnd 14: 2 dc in next st, *change to orange yarn*, dc in next st, 2 dc in next st, dc in next 2 st, *change to white yarn*, 2 dc in next st, 2 dc in next st, dc in next st, [2 dc in next st, dc in next st] 2 times – 18 st.

Fig. A

Fig. B

Fig. C

Rnds 15–17: (3 rounds) dc in each st around – 18 st.

Rnd 18: dc in next 3 st, *change to orange yarn*, dc in next 5 st, *change to white yarn*, dc in next 10 st – 18 st.

• Change to orange yarn.

Rnd 19: dc in each st around – 18 st.

• Change to dark grey yarn.

Rnd 20: dc in each st around – 18 st.

• Stuff head, and sew a mouth with black thread.

• Change to orange yarn.

Rnd 21: [2 dc in next st, dc in next 5 st] 3 times – 21 st.

Rnd 22: dc in each st around – 21 st.

Rnd 23: [2 dc in next st, dc in next 6 st] 3 times – 24 st.

Rnd 24: dc in each st around – 24 st.

• Change to dark grey yarn.

Rnd 25: [2 dc in next st, dc in next 7 st] 3 times – 27 st.

• Change to orange yarn.

Rnds 26–27: (2 rounds) dc in each st around – 27 st.

• Change to black yarn, leaving a piece of orange yarn about 40 cm long when you cut it.

To mark the feet: Find the stitch in round 27 that is in the front middle of the body. Then count back six stitches before that (not including the middle stitch) and mark this stitch.

Rnd 28: dc in each st around until you get to the marked stitch.

To make feet: Work a 3tr bob in each of next 4 st, dc in next 5 st, work a 3tr bob in each of next 4 st. Dc in each st around to the end of the round – 27 st.

• Make sure the bobbles that make up the feet are pushed outward.

• Stuff top half of body firmly.

Rnd 29: [dc2tog, dc in next st] 9 times – 18 st.

Rnd 30: [dc2tog, dc in next st] 6 times – 12 st.

Rnd 31: [dc2tog] 6 times – 6 st. FO, leaving a length of yarn.

• Thread the length of orange yarn out at the middle front of Poe at the top of round 23.

• Finish stuffing; stuff slightly less firmly below the waist.

• Neatly sew up the hole at the base with the length of black yarn and pull the yarn up through the body tightly to make sure the base lies flat before cutting the black yarn.

• To define the legs, take the orange yarn sticking out at the front middle, sew through the body from the top of round 24 (Fig. A–page 35) to the top of round 23 at the middle back (Fig. B–page 35) and pull tightly. Go down one round, then sew the yarn back through to the front and again pull tightly. (Fig. C–page 35) Continue to do this, working down the legs round by round, (Fig. D) until you reach the base of the figure. Take the yarn through the base (not tightly) a couple of times to secure and then cut it.

ARMS (make 2): Start with light beige yarn.

Rnd 1: ch 2, work 6 dc into first ch – 6 st.

Rnd 2: dc in each st around – 6 st.
• Change to dark grey yarn.

Rnd 3: [2 dc in next st, dc in next 2 st] 2 times – 8 st.

- Change to orange yarn.

Rnds 4–9: (6 rounds) dc in each st around – 8 st.

Rnd 10: [dc2tog, dc in next 2 st] 2 times – 6 st. Sl st in next st, then FO, leaving a length of yarn.

- Stuff the ends of the arms slightly, then sew the arms to the body.

GREY PANEL ON FRONT: Light grey yarn.

- Ch 3.

Row 1: skip first ch, then dc in next 2 ch, ch 1, turn.

Row 2: dc in next 2 st, FO, leaving a length of yarn.

- Sew to front of chest.

BLACK CABLE: Black yarn.

- Ch 6, FO, leaving a length of yarn.

- Sew one end under the grey panel, the other end two rounds below the belt on Poe's left side.

HELMET:

This is made in two halves that are sewn together in the middle, with a separate visor. Work tightly and carry the yarn you aren't using under the other yarn when you change colours.

Left side: Start with red yarn.

Rnd 1: ch 2, work 6 dc into first ch – 6 st.

Rnd 2: 2 dc in next st, *change to black yarn*, 2 dc in each of next 2 st, *change to red yarn*, 2 dc in next st, *change to black yarn*, 2 dc in each of next 2 st – 12 st.

Rnd 3: [2 dc in next st, dc in next st] 6 times – 18 st.

Fig. D

Fig. E

Fig. F

Rnd 4: dc in next 3 st, (sl st in next st, ch 2, tr in same st, *change to red yarn*, 2 tr in same st), dc in next 5 dc, (2 dc in next st, dc in next st) 4 times, dc in next st – 24 st.

You are now working in rows, not rounds. Continue working in the same direction for row 5.

Row 5: dc in next st, *change to black yarn*, dc in next 2 st, ch 1, turn.

Row 6: dc in next 16 st, *change to white yarn*, ch 1, turn.

Row 7: dc in next 16 st, *change to black yarn*, ch 1, turn.

Row 8: dc in next 16 st, ch 1, turn.

Row 9: dc in next 16 st, ch 1, turn – 16 st.

Row 10: dc in next 8 st, sl st in next 2 st. FO, leaving a length of yarn.

Right side: Start with red yarn.

Rnd 1: ch 2, work 6 dc into first ch – 6 st.

Rnd 2: 2 dc in each st around – 12 st.

• Change to black yarn.

Rnd 3: 2 dc in next st, dc in next st, 2 dc in next st, spike st over next st, 2 dc in next st, spike st over next st, (2 dc in next st, dc in next st) 3 times – 18 st.

Rnd 4: dc in next 4 st, *change to red yarn*, (dc in next st, 2 dc in next st) 4 times, dc in next 6 dc – 22 st.

You are now working in rows, not rounds. Continue working in the same direction for row 5.

Row 5: dc in next st, (tr in next st, *change to black yarn*, 2 tr in same st, ch 2, sl st in same st), dc in next 17 dc, ch 1, turn – 21 st.

Row 6: dc in next 16 st, ch 1, turn.

Row 7: dc in next 16 st, ch 1, turn.

Row 8: dc in next 16 st, ch 1, turn.

Row 9: dc in next 8 st, sl st in next 2 st. FO, leaving a length of yarn.

• Sew the two sides together neatly using the lengths of black yarn (the 3 tr in the same stitch are at the front). Weave in any loose ends. (Fig. E – page 37)

VISOR: Start with red yarn, leaving a length of yarn at the start.

• Ch 4.

Row 1: skip first ch, dc in next 3 ch, ch 1, turn – 3 st.

Row 2: dc in next st, 2 dc in next st, dc in next st, *change to black yarn*, ch 1, turn – 4 st.

Row 3: dc in next 4 st, ch 1, turn – 4 st.

Row 4: dc in next st, 2 dc in next st, dc in next 2 st, *change to red yarn*, ch 1, turn – 5 st.

Row 5: dc in next 5 st, ch 1, turn – 5 st.

Row 6: dc in next 2 st, 2 dc in next st, dc in next 2 st, *change to black yarn*, ch 1, turn – 6 st.

Row 7: dc in next 6 st, ch 1, turn – 6 st.

Row 8: dc in next 6 st, ch 1, turn – 6 st.

Row 9: dc in next st, *change to dark grey yarn*, dc in next 5 st, ch 1, turn – 6 st.

Row 10: dc in next 2 st, dc2tog, dc in next st, *change to black yarn*, dc in next st, ch 1, turn – 5 st.

Row 11: dc in next 5 st, ch 1, turn – 5 st.

Row 12: dc in next st, dc2tog, dc in next 2 st, *change to red yarn*, ch 1, turn – 4 st.

Row 13: dc in next 4 st, *change to black yarn*, ch 1, turn – 4 st.

Row 14: dc in next st, dc2tog, dc in next st – 3 st. FO, leaving a length of yarn.

• Using red yarn, sew three short lines that meet at the bottom on the grey section.

• Weave in ends (apart from the red and black ones at either end).

• Sew each end of the visor to the sides of the helmet, red end on the right, above the 3 tr in the same stitch. (Fig. F–page 37)

PROJECT 6

Kylo Ren

FINISHED SIZE: approximately 11 cm tall

Once a student of Luke Skywalker, Kylo Ren betrayed his Jedi training and turned to the dark side. He has honed his Force skills, becoming an expert in lightsaber combat and the power of mind control.

MATERIALS
See note on yarn, p. 6

- Black yarn (approx. 25 g)
- Dark grey yarn (approx. 5 g)
- Bright red yarn (approx. 5 g)
- Small amount of light grey yarn (for visor)
- 3.5 mm hook
- Tapestry needle
- Stuffing
- Drinking straw
- Stitch marker

HEAD AND BODY: Start with black yarn.

Rnd 1: ch 2, work 6 dc into first ch – 6 st.

Rnd 2: 2 dc in each st around – 12 st.

Rnd 3: [2 dc in next st, dc in next st] 6 times – 18 st.

Rnd 4: [2 dc in next st, dc in next 2 st] 6 times – 24 st.

Rnds 5–10: (6 rounds) dc in each st around – 24 st.

Rnd 11: [2 dc in next st, dc in next 3 st] 6 times – 30 st.

Rnd 12: dc in each st around – 30 st.

Rnd 13: in BLO, [dc2tog, dc in next 3 st] 6 times – 24 st.

Rnd 14: [dc2tog] 12 times – 12 st.

Rnd 15: [2 dc in next st, dc in next st] 6 times – 18 st.

Rnds 16–19: (4 rounds) dc in each st around – 18 st.

- Stuff head.
- Change to dark grey yarn.

Rnds 20–22: (3 rounds) dc in each st around – 18 st.

- Change to black yarn.

Rnd 23: [2 dc in next st, dc in next 5 st] 3 times – 21 st.

Rnd 24: dc in each st around – 21 st.

Rnd 25: [2 dc in next st, dc in next 6 st] 3 times – 24 st.

Rnd 26: dc in each st around – 24 st.

Rnd 27: [2 dc in next st, dc in next 7 st] 3 times – 27 st.

Rnd 28: dc in each st around – 27 st.

Rnd 29: [2 dc in next st, dc in next 8 st] 3 times – 30 st.

Rnd 30: dc in each st around – 30 st.

Fig. A

Fig. B

Fig. C

Fig. D

Rnd 31: in BLO, dc in next 12 st, 3tr bob in each of next 4 st, dc in next 5 st, 3tr bob in each of next 4 st, dc in next 5 st – 30 st.

- Make sure the bobbles that make up the feet are pushed outward.
- Stuff body.

Rnd 32: [dc2tog, dc in next st] 10 times – 20 st.

Rnd 33: [dc2tog, dc in next 2 st] 5 times – 15 st.

Rnd 34: [dc2tog, dc in next st] 5 times – 10 st.

Rnd 35: [dc2tog] 5 times – 5 st. FO, leaving a length of yarn.

Fig. E

- Finish stuffing firmly, then sew the hole at the base up neatly, and pull the yarn up tightly through the body to make sure the base lies flat. Take the yarn through the body again (not tightly) and then cut it. (Fig. A–page 41)

MASK:

This is made in two pieces, a visor and a mouthpiece, that are sewn onto the head.

VISOR: Light grey yarn.

- Ch 7.

Fig. F

Rnd 1: skip ch next to hook, 2 dc in next ch, dc in next 4 ch, 2 dc in next ch, work into other side of ch, 2 dc in same ch, dc in next 4 ch, 2 dc in next ch – 16 st.

Rnd 2: 2 dc in each of next 2 st, dc in next 4 st, 2 dc in each of next 4 st, dc in next 4 st, 2 dc in each of next 2 st – 24 st. Sl st in next st, then FO, leaving a length of yarn.

To make the black lines around the mask, work slip stitches along the surface into the holes between stitches.

- Insert your hook into one of the holes at the end of the original chain. Pull a loop of black yarn from underneath and through the hole, then work 5 sl st along the middle, pulling the yarn from underneath for each stitch. FO. (Fig. B–page 41)

- Turn the mask over. You will be working the following slip stitches along the wrong side to make a thinner line on the right side. Pulling the yarn from underneath as before, work a line of 17 slip stitches between rounds 1 and 2, forming an oval. FO.

- Still working on the wrong side and pulling the yarn from underneath, work a line of 25 slip stitches under the tops of round 2, forming an oval. FO. (Fig. C–page 41)

- Secure and cut all the ends of yarn on the wrong side of the mask, then sew the visor onto the head using the light grey yarn, positioning the top just below round 4 of the head. (Fig. D)

MOUTHPIECE: Black yarn.

Rnd 1: ch 2, work 6 dc into first ch – 6 st.

Rnd 2: 2 dc in each st around – 12 st.

Rnd 3: [2 dc in next st, dc in next 2 st] 4 times – 16 st.

Rnd 4: [dc in next 4 st, 2 dc in each of next 2 st, dc in next 2 st] 2 times – 20 st. Sl st in next st, then FO, leaving a length of yarn.

- Flatten this piece, then sew the edges together. (Fig. E) Pin into place on the grey part of the mask in a downward curve and sew securely on to the head.

Fig. G

Fig. H

Fig. I

Fig. J

Rnds 4–10: (7 rounds) in BLO, dc in each st around – 9 st.

Rnd 11: [dc2tog, dc in next st] 3 times – 6 st. Sl st in next st, then FO, leaving a length of yarn.

• Stuff the ends of the arms slightly, then sew the arms to the body.

CLOAK: Black yarn.

This consists of three parts: one that goes around the neck and two narrow triangular ends that hang down the back.

Left-hand back part:

• Ch 9, leaving a length of yarn at the start.

Row 1: dc in second ch from hook, dc in next ch, htr in next 3 ch, tr in next 3 ch, ch 2, turn – 8 st.

Row 2: tr in next 3 st, htr in next 3 st, dc in next st, sl st in next st – 8 st. FO.

Right-hand back part:

• Ch 8, leaving a length of yarn at the start.

Row 1: dc in second ch from hook, dc in next ch, htr in next 2 ch, tr in next 3 ch, ch 2, turn – 7 st.

Row 2: tr in next 3 st, htr in next 2 st, dc in next st, sl st in next st— 7 st. FO.

• Sew the longer triangle on the left-hand side of Kylo Ren's back, along the shortest side with point hanging down. (Fig. G–page 43) Sew the shorter triangle on the right-hand side, overlapping the other triangle. (Fig. H–page 43) Weave in ends.

HOOD: Black yarn.

• Ch 24.

Row 1: dc in second ch from hook, dc in next 22 ch, ch 1, turn – 23 st.

Rows 2–9: (8 rows) dc in next 23 st, ch 1, turn – 23 st.

Row 10: dc2tog, dc in next 7 st, dc2tog, dc in next st, dc2tog, dc in next 7 st, dc2tog, ch 1, turn – 19 st.

Row 11: dc2tog, dc in next 5 st, dc2tog, dc in next st, dc2tog, dc in next 5 st, dc2tog – 15 st. FO, leaving length of yarn.

• Fold in half and, using the length of yarn, sew up the back of the hood along the sides of rows 10 and 11 and then along the top of row 11. (Fig. F–page 42)

• Pin the bottom of the hood around the neck and sew in place.

ARMS (make 2): Black yarn.

Rnd 1: ch 2, work 6 dc into first ch – 6 st.

Rnd 2: dc in each st around – 6 st.

Rnd 3: [2 dc in next st, dc in next st] 3 times – 9 st.

Neck part:

• Ch 20.

Row 1: tr in third ch from hook, tr in next 17 ch. FO, leaving a length of yarn.

• With the initial chain at the top, pin in place all around the neck below the bottom of the hood, overlapping the tops of the arms and the back parts. Sew ends together, then sew along the initial chain and into the neck to secure. (Fig. I–page 43)

LIGHTSABER:

Main part: Start with bright red yarn.

Rnd 1: ch 2, work 6 dc into first ch – 6 st.

Rnds 2–12: (11 rounds) dc in each st around – 6 st.

• Change to black yarn.

Rnds 13–18: (6 rounds) dc in each st around – 6 st. FO, leaving a length of yarn.

Crossguard blades (make 2): Start with bright red yarn.

Rnd 1: ch 2, work 6 dc into first ch – 6 st.

Rnds 2–4: (3 rounds) dc in each st around – 6 st.

• Change to black yarn.

Rnd 5: dc in each st around – 6 st. Sl st in next st and FO, leaving a length of yarn.

• Cut 3 lengths of drinking straw to fit inside the parts of the lightsaber (if the straw is too wide, cut along it lengthways and roll it so it is thinner), and insert them.

• Sew up the end of the blade neatly; do not cut the yarn.

• Sew each of the crossguard blades to the side of the main handle just below the red part. (Fig. J)

• Sew to Kylo Ren's hand if you wish.

PROJECT 7

Obi-Wan Kenobi

FINISHED SIZE: approximately 9 cm tall

A Jedi who fought in the Clone Wars with Anakin Skywalker, Obi-Wan settled on Tatooine after the fall of the Jedi Order to watch over Luke Skywalker. After joining Luke to help the Rebel Alliance, he was struck down on the Death Star by Darth Vader, but his spirit lived on in the Force.

MATERIALS
See note on yarn, p. 6

- Light grey yarn (approx. 5 g)
- Pale peach yarn (approx. 5 g)
- Beige yarn (approx. 10 g)
- Brown yarn (approx. 15 g)
- Small amount of black embroidery thread (for mouth)
- Stuffing
- Pair of black plastic safety eyes (7.5 mm)
- 3.5 mm hook
- Tapestry needle
- Stitch marker

BEARD: Light grey yarn.

Row 1: ch 3, work 4 tr in first ch, ch 3, turn.

Row 2: skip ch next to hook, sl st in next 2 ch, dc in next tr, ch 4, skip next 2 tr, dc in next tr, ch 2, turn. (Fig. A)

Row 3: skip ch next to hook, sl st in next ch. FO, leaving a length of yarn.

HEAD AND BODY: Start with light grey yarn.

Rnd 1: ch 2, work 6 dc into first ch – 6 st.

Rnd 2: 2 dc in each st around – 12 st.

Rnd 3: [2 dc in next st, dc in next st] 6 times – 18 st.

Rnd 4: [2 dc in next st, dc in next 2 st] 6 times – 24 st.

Rnds 5–6: (2 rounds) dc in each st around – 24 st.

Rnd 7: *change to pale peach yarn*, dc in next 9 st, *change to light grey yarn*, dc in next 15 st – 24 st.

Rnd 8: *change to pale peach yarn*, dc in next 9 st, *change to light grey yarn*, dc in next 15 st – 24 st.

Rnd 9: *change to pale peach yarn*, dc in next 10 st, *change to light grey yarn*, dc in next 14 st – 24 st.

Rnd 10: *change to pale peach yarn*, dc in next 10 st, *change to light grey yarn*, dc in next 14 st – 24 st.

Rnd 11: *change to pale peach yarn*, dc in next 11 st, *change to light grey yarn*, dc in next 12 st, *change to pale peach yarn*, dc in next st – 24 st.

Rnd 12: [dc2tog, dc in next 2 st] 6 times – 18 st.

• Fit eyes between rounds 9 and 10, six stitches apart.

Fig. A

Fig. B

Fig. C

Rnd 13: [dc2tog, dc in next st] 6 times – 12 st.

- Change to brown yarn.

Rnd 14: [2 dc in next st, dc in next st] 6 times – 18 st.

- Change to beige yarn.

Rnd 15: dc in next 3 st, *change to brown yarn*, dc in next 3 st, *change to beige yarn*, dc in next 12 st – 18 st.

Rnd 16: dc in next 4 st, *change to brown yarn*, dc in next st, *change to beige yarn*, dc in next 13 st – 18 st.

Rnds 17–18: (2 rounds) dc in each st around – 18 st.

- Change to brown yarn.

Rnd 19: dc in each st around – 18 st.

- Stuff head.
- Pin the beard onto the face and sew in place with the loop of chains at the top making the moustache. The sections at the side join up to the hair. (Fig. B–page 47)
- Using black thread, sew a mouth so that it can be seen under the moustache. (Fig. C–page 47)
- Change to beige yarn.

Rnd 20: [2 dc in next st, dc in next 5 st] 3 times–21 st.

Rnd 21: dc in each st around – 21 st.

Rnd 22: [2 dc in next st, dc in next 6 st] 3 times – 24 st.

Rnd 23: dc in each st around – 24 st.

Rnd 24: [2 dc in next st, dc in next 7 st] 3 times – 27 st.

Rnds 25–26: (2 rounds) dc in each st around – 27 st.

- Change to brown yarn.

To mark the feet: Find the stitch in round 26 that is in the front middle of the body. Then count back six stitches before that (not including the middle stitch) and mark this stitch.

Rnd 27: in BLO for the whole round, dc in each st around until you get to the marked stitch.

To make feet: Work a 3tr bob in each of next 4 st, dc in next 5 st, work a 3tr bob in each of next 4 st. Dc in each st around to the end of the round – 27 st.

- Make sure the bobbles that make up the feet are pushed outward.
- Finish stuffing head and most of body firmly.

Rnd 28: [dc2tog, dc in next st] 9 times – 18 st.

Rnd 29: [dc2tog, dc in next st] 6 times – 12 st.

Rnd 30: [dc2tog] 6 times – 6 st. FO, leaving a length of yarn.

• Finish stuffing firmly, then sew the hole at the base up neatly, and pull the yarn up tightly through the body to make sure the base lies flat. Take the yarn through the body again (not tightly) and then cut it.

ARMS (make 2): Start with pale peach yarn.

Rnd 1: ch 2, work 6 dc into first ch – 6 st.

Rnd 2: sc in each st around – 6 st.

• Change to beige yarn.

Rnd 3: [2 dc in next st, dc in next st] 3 times – 9 st.

Rnds 4–6: (3 rounds) dc in each st around – 9 st.

Rnd 7: dc2tog, dc in next 7 st – 8 st.

Rnds 8–9: (2 rounds) dc in each st around – 8 st.

Rnd 10: [dc2tog, dc in next 2 st] 2 times – 6 st. Sl st in next st, then FO, leaving a length of yarn.

• Stuff the ends of the arms slightly, then sew the arms to the body.

ROBE: Brown yarn.

Start with the hood:

• Ch 24.

Row 1: dc in second ch from hook, dc in next 22 ch, ch 1, turn – 23 st.

Rows 2–9: (8 rows) dc in next 23 st, ch 1, turn – 23 st.

Row 10: dc2tog, dc in next 7 st, dc2tog, dc in next st, dc2tog, dc in next 7 st, dc2tog, ch 1, turn – 19 st.

Row 11: dc2tog, dc in next 5 st, dc2tog, dc in next st, dc2tog, dc in

Fig. D

Fig. E

Fig. F

next 5 st, dc2tog – 15 st. FO, leaving length of yarn.

• Fold in half and, using the length of yarn, sew up the back of the hood along the sides of rows 10 and 11 and then along the top of row 11. Weave in ends. (Fig. D–page 49)

Rest of robe:

Hold the hood upside down with the outside facing you and join in yarn to bottom of hood on the right.

Row 1: dc into the same point, then do 17 more dc, evenly spaced along the bottom of the hood. Ch 1, turn – 18 st.

Row 2: dc in next 2 st, ch 5, skip next 4 st, dc in next 6 st, ch 5, skip next 4 st, dc in next 2 st, ch 1, turn – 20 st.

Row 3: dc in next 2 st, work 5 dc around ch 5, dc in next 6 st, work 5 dc around ch 5, dc in next 2 st, ch 1, turn – 20 st.

Rows 4–6: (3 rows) dc in next 20 st, ch 1, turn – 20 st.

Row 7: 2 dc in next st, dc in next 5 st, 2 dc in next st, dc in next 6 st, 2 dc in next st, dc in next 5 st, 2 dc in next st, ch 1, turn – 24 st.

Rows 8–10: (3 rows) dc in next 24 st, ch 1, turn – 24 st.

Row 11: 2 dc in next st, dc in next 7 st, 2 dc in next st, dc in next 6 st, 2 sc in next st, dc in next 7 st, 2 dc in next st, ch 1, turn – 28 st.

Row 12: dc in next 28 st, ch 1, turn – 28 st.

Row 13: sl st in next 28 st, FO – 28 st. Weave in any loose ends.

SLEEVES (make 2):

• Ch 11.

Row 1: dc in second ch from hook, dc in next 9 ch, ch 1, turn – 10 st.

Row 2: dc in next 10 st, ch 1, turn – 10 st.

Row 3: 2 dc in next st, sc in next 8 st, 2 dc in next st, ch 1, turn – 12 st.

Row 4: dc in next 12 st, ch 1, turn – 12 st.

Row 5: 2 dc in next st, dc in next 10 st, 2 dc in next st, ch 1, turn – 14 st.

Row 6: dc in next 14 st, ch 1, turn – 14 st.

Row 7: 2 sc in next st, dc in next 12 st, 2 dc in next st, ch 1, turn – 16 st.

Row 8: dc in next 16 st – 16 st. FO, leaving length of yarn.

• Fold each sleeve in half and sew edges together, making a tube that is wider at one end than the other. (Fig. E–page 49) With the seam facing down, pin the narrower end of each sleeve into an armhole and sew in place. Weave in any loose ends. (Fig. F–page 49)

PROJECT 8

Lando Calrissian

FINISHED SIZE: approximately 9.5 cm tall

A charismatic smuggler and old friend of Han Solo, Lando won the mining colony at Bespin in a bet. He was a successful administrator of Cloud City until Darth Vader forced him to choose between the city and his friends. He then became a general in the Rebel Alliance, helping win the Battle of Endor.

MATERIALS
See note on yarn, p. 6

- Black yarn (approx. 15 g)
- Light brown yarn (approx. 10 g)
- Pale blue yarn (approx. 10 g)
- Gold yarn (approx. 5 g)
- Small amount of black embroidery thread (for mouth)
- 3.5 mm hook
- Tapestry needle
- Pair of black plastic safety eyes (7.5 mm)
- Stuffing
- Stitch marker

HEAD AND BODY: Start with light brown yarn.

Rnd 1: ch 2, work 6 dc into first ch – 6 st.

Rnd 2: 2 dc in each st around – 12 st.

Rnd 3: [2 dc in next st, dc in next st] 6 times – 18 st.

Rnd 4: [2 dc in next st, dc in next 2 st] 6 times – 24 st.

Rnds 5–11: (7 rounds) dc in each st around – 24 st.

Rnd 12: [dc2tog, dc in next 2 st] 6 times – 18 st.

• With the start of the round at the back, fit eyes between rounds 9 and 10, six stitches apart.

Rnd 13: [dc2tog, dc in next st] 6 times – 12 st.

• Change to black yarn.

Rnd 14: [2 dc in next st, dc in next st] 6 times – 18 st.

• Change to pale blue yarn.

Rnds 15–19: (5 rounds) dc in each st around – 18 st.

• Stuff head, and sew a mouth with black thread. (Fig. A)

• Using black yarn, sew a moustache and a short vertical line at the front middle of the neck over round 15. (Fig. B)

• Change to black yarn.

Rnd 20: dc in each st around – 18 st.

Rnd 21: [2 dc in next st, dc in next 5 st] 3 times – 21 st.

Rnd 22: dc in each st around – 21 st.

Rnd 23: [2 dc in next st, dc in next 6 st] 3 times – 24 st.

Rnd 24: dc in each st around – 24 st.

Rnd 25: [2 dc in next st, dc in next 7 st] 3 times – 27 st.

Fig. A

Fig. B

Fig.C

Fig. D

Fig. E

Rnds 26–27: (2 rounds) dc in each st around – 27 st.

To mark the feet: Find the stitch in round 27 that is in the front middle of the body. Then count back six stitches before that (not including the middle stitch) and mark this stitch.

Rnd 28: dc in each st around until you get to the marked stitch.

To make feet: Work a 3tr bob in each of next 4 st, dc in next 5 st, work a 3tr bob in each of next 4 st. Dc in each st around to the end of the round – 27 st.

• Make sure the bobbles that make up the feet are pushed outward.

• Stuff top half of body firmly.

Rnd 29: [dc2tog, dc in next st] 9 times – 18 st.

Rnd 30: [dc2tog, dc in next st] 6 times – 12 st.

Rnd 31: [dc2tog] 6 times – 6 st. FO, leaving a piece of yarn about 40 cm long.

• Finish stuffing; stuff slightly less firmly below the waist.

• Sew the hole at the base up neatly and then pull the yarn out at the middle front of Lando at the top of round 23. Pull the yarn up tightly to make sure the base lies flat.

• To define the legs, sew through the body from the top of round 24 to the top of round 23 at the middle back and pull tightly. Go down one round, then sew the yarn back through to the front and again pull tightly. Continue to do this, working down the legs round by round, until you reach the base of the figure. Take the yarn through the base (not tightly) a couple of times to secure and then cut it.

HAIR: Black yarn.

Rnd 1: ch 2, work 6 dc into first ch – 6 st.

Rnd 2: (2tr bob) 2 times in each st around – 12 st.

Rnd 3: [(2tr bob) 2 times in next st, 2tr bob in next st] 6 times – 18 st.

Rnd 4: 2tr bob in each st around – 18 st.

Stop working in rounds now and continue with row 5.

Row 5: ch 1, turn, htr in next 6 st, 2tr bob in next 3 st. FO, leaving a length of yarn. (The side facing you as you work this row is the outside of the hair.)

- Pin on to head with row 5 at the nape (it will stretch a little) and sew in place around edge, securing neatly in a few other places. (Fig. C–page 53)

ARMS (make 2): Start with light brown yarn.

Rnd 1: ch 2, work 6 dc into first ch – 6 st.

Rnd 2: dc in each st around – 6 st.

- Change to black yarn.

Rnd 3: [2dc in next st, dc in next 2 st] 2 times – 8 st.

- Change to pale blue yarn.

Rnd 4: dc in each st around – 8 st.

Rnds 5–9: (5 rounds) dc in each st around – 8 st.

Rnd 10: [dc2tog, dc in next 2 st] 2 times – 6 st. Sl st in next st, then FO, leaving a length of yarn.

- Stuff the ends of the arms slightly, then sew the arms to the body.

CLOAK: Start with gold yarn.

- Ch 10.

Row 1: dc in second ch from hook, sc in next 2 ch, htr in next 3 ch, tr in next 3 ch, *change to pale blue yarn*, ch 2, turn – 9 st.

Row 2: tr in next 3 st, htr in next 3 st, dc in next 3 st, ch 1, turn – 9 st.

Row 3: dc in next 3 st, htr in next 3 st, tr in next 3 st, ch 2, turn – 9 st.

Rows 4–11: Repeat rows 2 and 3 four times.

Row 12: tr in next 3 st, htr in next 3 st, dc in next 3 st, *change to gold yarn*, ch 1, turn – 9 st.

Row 13: dc in next 3 st, htr in next 3 st, tr in next 3 st, ch 1, turn – 9 st.

Row 14: sl st in next 9 st – 9 st. FO.

- To make the collar, hold the cloak with the right side facing you (first row to the right). Join in black yarn to top right. Dc along the top into the ends of the rows (approx. 13 st), ch 1, turn. Dc in BLO of previous black row. (Fig. D) FO, leaving a length of yarn, and use this to sew cloak above shoulders. (Fig. E) Weave in all other loose ends.

Admiral Ackbar

FINISHED SIZE: approximately 10 cm tall

Admiral Ackbar comes from the planet Mon Calamari and was the commander of the rebel fleet for the attack on the second Death Star, famously announcing that "It's a trap!" He's now a respected senior leader of the Resistance.

MATERIALS
See note on yarn, p. 6

- Russet yarn (approx. 10 g)
- White yarn (approx. 10 g)
- Cream yarn (approx. 5 g)
- Small amounts of yellow and grey yarn (for uniform details)
- Small amount of black embroidery thread (for mouth)
- 3.5 mm hook
- Tapestry needle
- Pair of yellow or amber plastic safety eyes (10.5 mm)
- Stuffing
- Stitch marker

Fig. A

EYE BUMPS (make 2): Russet yarn.

• Ch 2, work 8 dc into first ch, sl st into first sc, FO, leaving length of yarn. Don't tighten the hole at the centre. (Fig. A)

HEAD AND BODY: Start with russet yarn.

Rnd 1: ch 2, work 6 dc into first ch – 6 st.

Rnd 2: 2 dc in each st around – 12 st.

Rnd 3: [(2 dc in next st) 3 times, dc in next 3 st] 2 times – 18 st.

Rnd 4: dc in next 2 st, [2 dc in next st] 3 times, dc in next 6 st, [2 dc in next st] 3 times, dc in next 4 st – 24 st.

Rnds 5–6: (2 rounds) dc in each st around – 24 st.

Rnd 7: dc in next 16 st, [2 dc in next st] 3 times, dc in next 5 st – 27 st.

Rnds 8–9: (2 rounds) dc in each st around – 27 st.

Rnd 10: dc in next 17 st, tr in next st, dc in next 3 st, tr in next st, tr in next 5 st – 27 st.

Rnd 11: dc in each st around – 27 st.

Rnd 12: dc in next 3 st, [dc2tog] 3 times, dc in next 18 st – 24 st.

Rnd 13: [dc2tog, dc in next 2 st] 6 times – 18 st.

• Fit eyes on either side of the head between rounds 10 and 11. The tr stitches you made on round 10 form part of the nostrils, so they show the front of the head, and the eyes go four stitches on either side of them. Insert each safety eye through an eye bump first, then push though head and fix washer on the inside of the head. (Figs. B, C & D)

Fig. B

Fig. C

Fig. D

Fig. E

Fig. F

Rnd 14: dc in next 9 st, [dc2tog] 3 times, dc in next 3 st – 15 st.

Rnd 15: dc in each st around – 15 st.

• Change to cream yarn.

Rnd 16: [2 dc in next st, dc in next 4 st] 3 times – 18 st.

Rnd 17a: in FLO, dc in each st around – 18 st. Sl st into next st and FO.

• Push the nostril bumps outward and stuff head. Using black thread, embroider the mouth and little lines next to the nostril bumps to make nostrils.

• Neaten up the ends of yarn from the eye bumps.

Continue with the body:

• Push round 17a upward to make the collar, then join in cream yarn at back into the back loops left from round 16.

Rnd 17b: in BLO, dc in each st around – 18 st.

Rnds 18–21: (4 rounds) dc in each st around – 18 st.

• Find the stitch in round 21 that is in the front middle, then count back four stitches before that (not including the middle stitch) and mark this stitch.

Rnd 22: dc in each st around until you get to the marked stitch, [3tr bob in next st, dc in next st] 5 times, then treat as end of round.

• Make sure the bobbles that make up the belt are pushed outward.

Continue to make bottom of tunic, back part:

• In FLO, dc in next 8 st, ch1, turn.

• Dc in next 8 st, ch1, turn.

• Dc in next 8 st, FO.

Continue to make bottom of tunic, front part:

• Join in yarn to front loop of first dc after first bobble st.

• In FLO, dc in next 8 st, ch1, turn.

• Dc in next 8 st, FO.

• Use grey yarn to sew a small rectangular shape on top left-hand side of chest.

Continue to make trousers: White yarn.

• Join in yarn at back of body into back loops left from round 22. (Fig. E)

Rnd 23: in BLO, [2 dc in next st, dc in next 5 st] 3 times – 21 st.

Rnd 24: dc in each st around – 21 st.

Rnd 25: [2 dc in next st, dc in next 6 st] 3 times – 24 st.

Rnd 26: dc in each st around – 24 st.

Rnd 27: [2 dc in next st, dc in next 7 st] 3 times – 27 st.

Rnds 28–29: (2 rounds) dc in each st around – 27 st.

To mark the feet: Find the stitch in round 29 that is in the front middle of the body. Then count back six stitches before that (not including the middle stitch) and mark this stitch.

Rnd 30: dc in each st around until you get to the marked stitch.

To make feet: (Fig. F) Work a 3tr bob in each of next 4 st, dc in next 5 st, work a 3tr bob in each of next 4 st. Dc in each st around to the end of the round – 27 st.

• Make sure the bobbles that make up the feet are pushed outward.

• Finish stuffing head and stuff top half of body firmly.

• Neaten up any loose ends of yarn on the collar and the tunic.

Rnd 31: [dc2tog, dc in next st] 9 times – 18 st.

Rnd 32: [dc2tog, dc in next st] 6 times – 12 st.

Rnd 33: [dc2tog] 6 times – 6 st. FO, leaving a piece of yarn about 40 cm long.

• Finish stuffing; stuff slightly less firmly below the waist.

• Use yellow yarn to sew a line down the side of each leg between rounds 23 and 29, sewing over each round.

• Sew the hole at the base up neatly and then pull the yarn out at the middle front of Admiral Ackbar at the top of round 25. Pull the yarn up tightly to make sure the base lies flat.

• To define the legs, sew through the body from the top of round 26 to the top of round 25 at the middle back and pull tightly. Go down one round, then sew the yarn back through to the front and again pull tightly. Continue to do this, working down the legs round by round, until you reach the base of the figure. Take the yarn through the base (not tightly) a couple of times to secure and then cut it.

ARMS (make 2): Start with russet yarn.

Rnd 1: ch 2, work 6 dc into first ch – 6 st.

Rnd 2: dc in each st around – 6 st.

Rnd 3: [2 dc in next st, dc in next st] 3 times – 9 st.

Rnd 4: dc in each st around – 9 st.

Rnd 5: dc2tog, dc in next 7 st – 8 st.

• Change to white yarn.

Rnds 6–10: (5 rounds) dc in each st around – 8 st.

Rnd 11: [dc2tog, dc in next 2 st] 2 times – 6 st. Sl st in next st, then FO, leaving a length of yarn.

• Stuff the ends of the arms slightly, then sew the arms to the body.

Nien Nunb

FINISHED SIZE: approximately 10 cm tall

Nien Nunb is a Sullustan who co-piloted the *Millennium Falcon* with Lando Calrissian in the attack on the second Death Star. He is still active in the Resistance as an X-wing pilot, fighting in and surviving the Battle at Starkiller Base.

MATERIALS
See note on yarn, p. 6

- Pale peach yarn (approx. 10 g)
- Orange yarn (approx. 10 g)
- Black yarn (approx. 5 g)
- Dark beige yarn (approx. 5 g)
- Small amount of black embroidery thread (for mouth)
- 3.5 mm hook
- 4.0 mm hook
- Tapestry needle
- Pair of black plastic safety eyes (9 mm)
- Stuffing
- Stitch marker

HEAD AND BODY: Start with pale peach yarn.

Rnd 1: ch 2, work 6 dc into first ch – 6 st.

Rnd 2: 2 dc in each st around – 12 st.

Rnd 3: [2 dc in next st, dc in next 3 st] 3 times – 15 st.

Rnd 4: [2 dc in next st, dc in next 4 st] 3 times – 18 st.

Rnd 5: [2 dc in next st, dc in next 5 st] 3 times – 21 st.

Rnd 6: [2 dc in next st, dc in next 6 st] 3 times – 24 st.

Rnds 7–8: (2 rounds) dc in each st around – 24 st.

Rnd 9 including jowls:

Rnd 9a: dc in next 4 st, (FLO: dc in next st, htr in next st, tr in next 3 st, htr in next st, dc in next st), dc in both loops of next st, (FLO: dc in next st, htr in next st, tr in next 3 st, htr in next st, dc in next st), ch 1, turn – 19 st. (Fig. A)

Fig. A

Rnd 9b: dc in next 7 back loops (the unworked back loops of rnd 8), dc in next st in both loops, dc in next 6 back loops, sl st in next back loop, ch 1, turn – 15 st. (Fig. B)

Fig. B

Rnd 9c: (FLO: dc in next st, htr in next st, tr in next 3 st, htr in next st, dc in next st, sl st in next st, dc in next st, htr in next st, tr in next 3 st, htr in next st, dc in next st), dc in both loops of next 5 st, back to start of round – 20 st. (Fig. C)

Fig. C

Rnd 10: dc in next 4 st, dc in next 15 back loops (remaining from working in front loops previously), dc in next 5 st – 24 st.

Rnd 11: dc in each st around – 24 st.

Rnd 12: [dc2tog, dc in next 2 st] 6 times – 18 st.

Fig. D

Fig. E

Fig. F

- Fit eyes between rounds 6 and 7, five stitches apart, centred above jowls. (Fig. D – page 61)

Rnd 13: [dc2tog, dc in next st] 6 times – 12 st.

- Change to orange yarn, leaving a length of pale peach yarn when you cut it.

Rnd 14: [dc in next st, 2 dc in next st] 6 times – 18 st.

- Stuff head, sew mouth, and, using the length of pale peach yarn, secure the edges of the jowls with a couple of stitches per layer on each side.

- Change to black yarn.

Rnds 15–18: (4 rounds) dc in next 7 st, *change to orange yarn*, dc in next 4 st, *change to black yarn*, dc in next 7 st – 18 st.

Rnd 19: dc in each st around – 18 st.

- Change to orange yarn.

Rnd 20: [2 dc in next st, dc in next 5 st] 3 times – 21 st.

Rnd 21: dc in each st around – 21 st.

Rnd 22: [2 dc in next st, dc in next 6 st] 3 times – 24 st.

Rnd 23: dc in each st around – 24 st.

Rnd 24: [2 dc in next st, dc in next 7 st] 3 times – 27 st.

- Change to black yarn, leaving a piece of orange yarn about 30 cm long when you cut it.

Rnds 25–26: (2 rounds) dc in each st around – 27 st.

To mark the feet: Find the stitch in round 26 that is in the front middle of the body. Then count back six stitches before that (not including the middle stitch) and mark this stitch.

Rnd 27: dc in each st around until you get to the marked stitch.

To make feet: Work a 3tr bob in each of next 4 st, dc in next 5 st, work a 3tr bob in each of next 4 st. Dc in each st around to the end of the round – 27 st.

- Make sure the bobbles that make up the feet are pushed outward.

- Stuff top half of body firmly.

Rnd 28: [dc2tog, dc in next st] 9 times – 18 st.

Rnd 29: [dc2tog, dc in next st] 6 times – 12 st.

Rnd 30: [dc2tog] 6 times – 6 st. FO, leaving a piece of yarn about 30 cm long.

- Thread the length of orange yarn out at the middle front of Nien Nunb at the top of round 22.

- Finish stuffing; stuff slightly less firmly below the waist.

- Neatly sew up the hole at the base with the length of black yarn and pull the yarn out at the middle front of Nien Nunb at the top of round 25. Pull the yarn up tightly to make sure the base lies flat.

- To define the legs, take the orange yarn sticking out at the front middle, sew through the body from the top of round 23 to the top of round 22 at the middle back and pull tightly. Go down one round, then sew the yarn back through to the front and again pull tightly. Continue to do this, working down the legs round by round, until you reach the black part of the figure. Secure and cut the orange yarn, then change to the black yarn and continue as before until you reach the base of the figure. Take the yarn through the base (not tightly) a couple of times to secure and then cut it.

ARMS (make 2): Start with black yarn.

Rnd 1: ch 2, work 6 dc into first ch – 6 st.

Rnd 2: dc in each st around – 6 st.

Rnd 3: [2dc in next st, dc in next st] 3 times – 9 st.

Rnd 4: dc in each st around – 9 st.

- Change to orange yarn.

Rnd 5: dc2tog, dc in next 7 st – 8 st.

Rnds 6–9: (4 rounds) dc in each st around – 8 st.

Rnd 10: [dc2tog, dc in next 2 st] 2 times – 6 st. Sl st in next st, then FO, leaving a length of yarn.

- Stuff the ends of the arms slightly, then sew the arms to the body.

CAP: Dark beige yarn. Use 4.0 mm hook or work more loosely.

Rnd 1: ch 2, work 6 dc into first ch – 6 st.

Rnd 2: 2 dc in each st around – 12 st.

Rnd 3: [2 dc in next st, dc in next 3 st] 3 times – 15 st.

Rnd 4: [2 dc in next st, dc in next 4 st] 3 times – 18 st.

Rnd 5: [2 dc in next st, dc in next 5 st] 3 times – 21 st.

You are now working in rows, not rounds. Continue working in the same direction for row 6.

Row 6: ch 6, turn, dc into second ch from hook, dc in next 3 ch, skip last ch, sl st in last dc on previous round, dc in next st, sl st in next st, dc in next 12 st, ch 6, turn.

Row 7: dc into second ch from hook, dc in next 3 ch, skip last ch, sl st in last dc on previous row, dc in next st, sl st in next st, dc in next 8 st, ch 1, turn.

Rows 8–10: (3 rows) dc in next 7 st, ch 1, turn.

Row 11: 2 dc in next st, dc in next 5 st, 2 dc in next st. FO, leaving length of yarn about 30 cm long. (Fig. E)

- Sew the end of each ch 6 strip to either side of the back (Row 11) to make ear holes; do not cut yarn. (Fig. F)

EARS (make 2): Pale peach yarn.

- Ch 3, work 5 htr into first ch. Work over the initial length of yarn and pull this tight to close the hole at the centre. FO, leaving length of yarn.

- Sew to sides of head, making sure the cap will fit over the ears.

- Sew cap to head around the edge in a few places to secure it.

Cantina Band

FINISHED SIZE: approximately 10 cm tall

Figrin D'an and the Modal Nodes play their popular music in the cantina in Mos Eisley on Tatooine. They keep the mood light and pleasant . . . no matter what kind of disruption is happening in the cantina.

MATERIALS
See note on yarn, p. 6

- Pale peach yarn (approx. 10 g)
- Black yarn (approx. 10 g)
- Dark grey yarn (approx. 5 g)
- Small amounts of beige and light grey yarn (for instruments)
- 3.5 mm hook
- Tapestry needle
- Pair of black plastic safety eyes (10.5 mm)
- Stuffing
- 1 or 2 drinking straws
- Stitch marker

HEAD AND BODY: Start with pale peach yarn.

Rnd 1: ch 2, work 6 dc into first ch – 6 st.

Rnd 2: 2 dc in each st around – 12 st.

Rnd 3: [2 dc in next st, dc in next st] 6 times – 18 st.

Rnd 4: [2 dc in next st, dc in next 2 st] 6 times – 24 st.

Rnd 5: [2 dc in next st, dc in next 7 st] 3 times – 27 st.

Rnds 6–9: (4 rounds) dc in each st around – 27 st.

Rnd 10: [dc2tog, dc in next 7 st] 3 times – 24 st.

Rnd 11: [dc2tog, dc in next 6 st] 3 times – 21 st.

Rnds 12–13: (2 rounds) dc in each st around – 21 st.

Rnd 14: dc in next st, dc2tog, dc in next st, [in FLO, dc in next st, htr in each of next 3 st, dc in next st, sl st in each of next 2 st, dc in next st, htr in each of next 3 st, dc in next st]; working in both loops, dc2tog, dc in next st, dc2tog – 18 st.

• Fit eyes between rounds 11 and 12, five stitches apart, with the 2 sl st in round 14 in the middle below them. (Fig. A)

Rnd 15: dc2tog, dc in next st, [in BLO (the back loops remaining from working in front loops of Rnd 14), (Fig. B) dc2tog, dc in next st, dc2tog, 2tr bob in each of next 2 st, dc2tog, dc in next st, dc2tog]; working in both loops, dc2tog, dc in next st – 12 st.

• Push bobble stitches outwards.

• Change to black yarn.

Rnd 16: dc in each st around – 12 st.

Fig. A

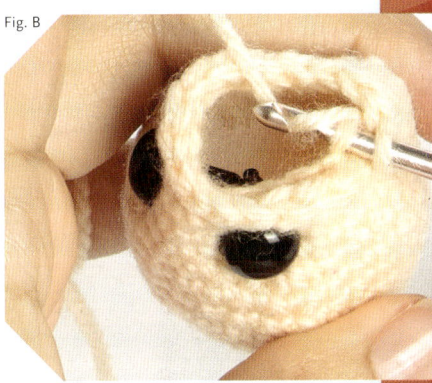
Fig. B

Fig. C

Rnd 17: [2 dc in next st, dc in next 3 st] 3 times – 15 st.

Rnd 18: [2 dc in next st, dc in next 4 st] 3 times – 18 st.

Rnds 19–22: (4 rounds) dc in each st around – 18 st.

• Stuff head, and, using pale peach yarn, sew a vertical line between the eyes, from the top of round 12 to the top of round 5, pulling it a little tight. Secure yarn.

• Change to dark grey yarn.

Rnd 23: [2 dc in next st, dc in next 5 st] 3 times – 21 st.

Rnd 24: dc in each st around – 21 st.

Rnd 25: [2 dc in next st, dc in next 6 st] 3 times – 24 st.

Rnd 26: dc in each st around – 24 st.

Rnd 27: [2 dc in next st, dc in next 7 st] 3 times – 27 st.

• Change to black yarn.

Rnds 28–29: (2 rounds) dc in each st around – 27 st.

To mark the feet: Find the stitch in round 29 that is in the front middle of the body. Then count back six stitches before that (not including the middle stitch) and mark this stitch.

Rnd 30: dc in each st around until you get to the marked stitch.

To make feet: Work a 3tr bob in each of next 4 st, dc in next 5 st, work a 3tr bob in each of next 4 st. Dc in each st around to the end of the round – 27 st.

• Make sure the bobbles that make up the feet are pushed outward.

• Stuff top half of body firmly.

Rnd 31: [dc2tog, dc in next st] 9 times – 18 st.

Rnd 32: [dc2tog, dc in next st] 6 times – 12 st.

Rnd 33: [dc2tog] 6 times – 6 st. FO, leaving a piece of yarn about 40 cm long.

• Finish stuffing; stuff slightly less firmly below the waist.

• Sew the hole at the base up neatly and then pull the yarn out at the middle front of the figure at the top of round 25. Pull the yarn up tightly to make sure the base lies flat.

• To define the legs, sew through the body from the top of round 26 to the top of round 25 at the middle back and pull tightly. Go down one round, then sew the yarn back through to the front and again pull tightly. Continue to do this, working down the legs round by round, until you reach the base of the figure. Take the yarn through the base (not tightly) a couple of times to secure and then cut it.

ARMS (make 2): Start with pale peach yarn.

Rnd 1: ch 2, work 6 dc into first ch – 6 st.

Rnd 2: dc in each st around – 6 st.

• Change to black yarn, leaving a length of pale peach yarn when you cut it. Thread this yarn out through the hand.

Rnd 3: [2dc in next st, dc in next 2 st] 2 times – 8 st.

Rnds 4–9: (6 rounds) dc in each st around – 8 st.

Rnd 10: [dc2tog, dc in next 2 st] 2 times – 6 st. Sl st in next st, then FO, leaving a length of yarn.

- Stuff the ends of the arms slightly, then sew the arms to the body. (Fig. C–page 65)

MUSICAL INSTRUMENTS:

FANFAR: Beige yarn.

Rnd 1: ch 2, work 6 dc into first ch – 6 st.

Rnds 2–8: (7 rounds) dc in each st around – 6 st. FO, leaving a length of yarn.

FIZZ: Black yarn.

Rnd 1: ch 2, work 6 dc into first ch – 6 st.

Rnds 2–10: (9 rounds) dc in each st around – 6 st. FO, leaving a length of yarn.

KLOO HORN: Light grey yarn.

Rnd 1: ch 2, work 6 dc into first ch – 6 st.

Rnds 2–12: (11 rounds) dc in each st around – 6 st. FO, leaving a length of yarn.

- Cut lengths of drinking straws to fit inside each of the instruments. If the straw is too wide, cut along it lengthways and roll it so it is thinner, and insert the pieces into the instruments.

- For the Fizz (black), take some light grey yarn and sew around in a circle between rounds 7 and 8, then sew a vertical line along the side.

- For the Kloo Horn (grey), take a length of black yarn and sew it securely so it sticks out of the middle of the first round.

FANFAR

FIZZ

KLOO HORN

BANDFILL

- Sew up the ends neatly. Cut the grey yarn, but leave all the other lengths of yarn. Sew each instrument to the mouth of a band member, leaving a short length of yarn showing for the Fanfar (beige) and Fizz (black), and a longer length for the Kloo Horn (grey instrument).

BANDFILL: Make in three parts

Part one: Beige yarn.

Rnd 1: ch 2, work 7 dc into first ch – 7 st.
Rnd 2: 2 dc in each st around – 14 st.
Rnd 3: dc in next 7 st, (sl st in next st, ch 4, skip 2 ch next to hook, sl st in next 2 ch, sl st back into same st on round), dc in next 6 st – 14 st.

- For rounds following ones with the sticking-out part, work into the first sl st, take the yarn under the part, skip the second sl st and then work into the next st on the round.

Rnd 4: dc in each st around – 14 st.
Rnds 5–8: (4 rounds) repeat rounds 3 and 4 two times.
Rnd 9: dc in each st around – 14 st.
Rnd 10: [dc2tog] 7 times – 7 st. FO.

- Stuff slightly and sew up hole at bottom neatly.

Part two: Light grey yarn.

- Ch 3, work 8 htr into first ch. Work over the initial length of yarn and pull this tight. Sl st into first htr to join. FO, leaving length of yarn.

- Sew to front of instrument.

Part three: Light grey yarn.

- Ch 4, skip ch next to hook, sl st in next 3 ch. FO, leaving a length of yarn.

- Sew to the beige part of the instrument on round 2, just above the parts sticking out. Take the yarn back out of the top and use this to sew it to the mouth.

- Using the lengths of pale peach yarn, sew the hands of each band member in place on their instruments.

GREEDO

FINISHED SIZE: approximately 10 cm tall

This Rodian bounty hunter was keen to collect the bounty that Jabba the Hutt had posted on Han Solo. He caught up with Han in the Mos Eisley cantina, but the smuggler was ready for him and Greedo never made it out alive.

MATERIALS
See note on yarn, p. 6

- Sage green yarn (approx. 10 g)
- Turquoise yarn (approx. 10 g)
- Light orange yarn (approx. 5 g)
- Light grey yarn (approx. 5 g)
- Small amount of pale yellow yarn (for uniform details)
- 3.5 mm hook
- Tapestry needle
- Pair of black plastic safety eyes (9 mm)
- Stuffing
- Stitch marker

HEAD AND BODY: Start with sage green yarn.

Rnd 1: ch 2, work 6 dc into first ch – 6 st.

Rnd 2: 2 dc in each st around – 12 st.

Rnd 3: [2 dc in next st, dc in next st] 6 times – 18 st.

Rnd 4: [2 dc in next st, dc in next 2 st] 6 times – 24 st.

Rnds 5–7: (3 rounds) dc in each st around – 24 st.

Rnd 8: dc in next 11 st, 2 dc in next st, dc in next 12 st – 25 st.

• Insert stitch marker between the twelfth and thirteenth stitches of round 8.

Rnd 9: dc in next 12 st, 2 dc in next st, dc in next 12 st – 26 st.

Rnd 10: dc in next 12 st, 2 dc in next 2 st, dc in next 12 st – 28 st.

Rnd 11: dc in next 13 st, 2 dc in next 2 st, dc in next 13 st – 30 st.

Rnd 12: dc in next st, [dc2tog, dc in next st] 3 times, dc2tog 7 times, [dc in next st, dc2tog] 2 times – 18 st.

• Fit eyes between rounds 7 and 8, four stitches apart, with the stitch marker showing the midpoint between the eyes. (Fig. A)

Rnd 13: dc in next 2 st, dc2tog, dc in next 2 st, dc2tog 4 times, dc in next 2 st, dc2tog – 12 st.

• Change to turquoise yarn.

Rnd 14: dc in each st around – 12 st.

• Change to orange yarn.

Rnd 15: [dc in next st, 2 dc in next st] 3 times, *change to turquoise yarn*, dc in next st, 2 dc in next st, *change to orange yarn*, [dc in next st, 2 dc in next st] 2 times – 18 st.

• Stuff head.

Fig. A

Fig. B

Fig. C

Fig. D

Fig. E

Fig. F

Fig. G

Rnds 16–19: (4 rounds) dc in next 9 st, *change to turquoise yarn*, dc in next 3 st, *change to orange yarn*, dc in next 6 st – 18 st.

Rnd 20: dc in next 9 st, *change to light grey yarn*, dc in next 3 st, *change to orange yarn*, dc in next 6 st – 18 st.

• Change to turquoise yarn.

Rnd 21: [2 dc in next st, dc in next 5 st] 3 times – 21 st.

Rnd 22: dc in each st around – 21 st.

Rnd 23: [2 dc in next st, dc in next 6 st] 3 times – 24 st.

Rnd 24: dc in each st around – 24 st.

Rnd 25: [2 dc in next st, dc in next 7 st] 3 times – 27 st.

Rnds 26–27: (2 rounds) dc in each st around – 27 st.

• Change to light grey yarn, leaving a piece of turquoise yarn about 40 cm long when you cut it.

To mark the feet: Find the stitch in round 27 that is in the front middle of the body. Then count back six stitches before that (not including the middle stitch) and mark this stitch.

Rnd 28: dc in each st around until you get to the marked stitch.

To make feet: Work a 3tr bob in each of next 4 st, dc in next 5 st, work a 3tr bob in each of next 4 st. Dc in each st around to the end of the round—27 st.

• Make sure the bobbles that make up the feet are pushed outward.

• Stuff top half of body firmly.

Rnd 29: [dc2tog, dc in next st] 9 times – 18 st.

Rnd 30: [dc2tog, dc in next st] 6 times – 12 st.

Rnd 31: [dc2tog] 6 times – 6 st. FO, leaving a length of yarn.

• Thread the length of turquoise yarn out at the middle front of Greedo at the top of round 23.

• Using a double strand of pale yellow yarn, sew a line up the side of each leg, sewing over a couple of rounds at a time.

- Finish stuffing; stuff slightly less firmly below the waist.
- Neatly sew up the hole at the base with the length of light grey yarn and pull the yarn up through the body tightly to make sure the base lies flat before cutting the light grey yarn.
- To define the legs, take the turquoise yarn sticking out at the front middle, sew through the body from the top of round 24 to the top of round 23 at the middle back, and pull tightly. Go down one round, then sew the yarn back through to the front and again pull tightly. Continue to do this, working down the legs round by round, until you reach the base of the figure. Take the yarn through the base (not tightly) a couple of times to secure and then cut it.

MOUTH: Sage green yarn.

- Ch 2, work 6 dc into first ch. Join to first dc with a sl st. Do not pull the centre tight. FO, leaving length of yarn.

- Flatten into an oval shape and sew to the front of the head over the bump at the bottom of the face. (Fig. B–page 71)

ANTENNAE (make 2): Sage green yarn.

- Ch 3, sl st in second ch from hook, work 6 dc into next ch, working over the initial tail of yarn. Join to first dc with a sl st and pull tail of yarn to close hole. FO, leaving length of yarn.

- Sew to top of head. (Fig. C–page 71)

EARS (make 2): Sage green yarn.

- Ch 4, skip ch next to hook, sl st in next ch, skip next ch, 2 htr in first ch, ch 1, tr in first ch. FO, leaving length of yarn.

- Sew to sides of head. (Fig. D–page 71)

CREST: Sage green yarn.

To make the crest on the back of Greedo's head, thread a length of sage green yarn onto your needle and take the yarn through the back of the head, between rounds 2 and 3, leaving a short length of yarn sticking out. Sew a stitch in the same place. Insert the needle a round below and leave a short loop of yarn, (Fig. E–page 72) then sew a stitch in the same place to secure it. Keep doing this in a vertical line along the back of the head until you get to the bottom. Cut each loop and trim to length. (Fig. F–page 72)

ARMS (make 2): Start with sage green yarn.

Rnd 1: ch 2, work 6 dc into first ch – 6 st.

Rnd 2: dc in each st around – 6 st.

- Change to turquoise yarn.

Rnd 3: [2dc in next st, dc in next 2 st] 2 times – 8 st.

Rnds 4–9: (6 rounds) dc in each st around – 8 st.

Rnd 10: [dc2tog, dc in next 2 st] 2 times – 6 st. Sl st in next st, then FO, leaving a length of yarn.

- Using a double strand of pale yellow yarn, sew a line up each arm, sewing over a couple of rounds at a time. (Fig. G–page 72)

- Stuff the ends of the arms slightly, then sew the arms to the body.

About the Author

Lucy Collin learned to crochet as a child, when she was taught by her grandmother. But it wasn't until she had children of her own and discovered she could use her slightly rusty crochet skills to create amigurumi characters and cute toys that her obsession was born. Now, Lucy has combined her passion for designing creatures and characters with her love of science fiction and fantasy. She has published patterns in magazines such as *Inside Crochet* and *Crochet Gifts*, and she created the patterns for the book *Hollywood Crochet* and the first *Star Wars Crochet* book. Find Lucy on Etsy as Lucyravenscar (lucyravenscar.etsy.com) or follow her on her blog (lucyravenscar.blogspot.com). Lucy lives in West Sussex, England.

Acknowledgements

Thank you to all my family and friends for encouraging me with my crochet, and especially to my husband and sons for loving *Star Wars* with me and helping with my design inspiration.